LET'S TRAVEL THE WORLD

A TRAVEL GUIDE AND TIPS FOR THE 21ST CENTURY

NIKKI PAGE

CONTENTS

ACKNOWLEDGMENTS

To my fans, fellow travelers, and social media friends, thank you for telling me what you wanted to read about. Your support over the years has been invaluable.

Thank you to the team of editors and design artists. You took my words and turned them into an absolutely beautiful book.

To my publishing company, Viva Purpose which has invested its time and money into my dream, thank you for believing in me.

To my husband, Steve, thank you for bringing me coffee during the long hours of writing and creating. Mostly, thank you for still loving me during this process, I know it can be hard.

FOREWORD

Traveling is an excellent way to expand personal growth and learn about the world around you. I've learned more during my travels than in any classroom. For me, one of the biggest hurdles was finding a travel partner, and it wasn't until I was in my forties that I finally figured out that I didn't need one.

I had been dreaming of a trip to Belize. And like many of us with dreams, I talked endlessly about this trip I would someday embark on. But a friend of mine, Mike, finally pushed me over the edge. One evening, I was sharing pictures of the Great Barrier Reef and the Blue Hole in Belize. I was talking, once again with excitement about what Belize had to offer when Mike made a quick, off-hand comment, which changed my life. He said, "So, what are you waiting for?". And in that moment, when I heard the answer in my head - the answer being, "I am waiting for someone to go with me" – I knew I didn't need to wait. I didn't even get the words out. I was stunned into saying something like; "I don't know, I guess I should just go." And why shouldn't I? I had moved to California at eighteen, alone. I raised my two kids, alone. Why on earth was I waiting for a friend or a partner to travel with? What was I thinking? So, that was that. I went home, started planning, and in just a few months I was in Belize!

Today, traveling solo is my "go-to" way of traveling, simply for the freedom to go when and where I want. I've traveled for weeks and months at a time, with my longest stretch being over a ten-month period and I've crisscrossed the United States by train racking up over ten thousand miles on Amtrak. No matter how long your trip, where you are traveling to, or whom you are traveling with, planning to take those first few trips can be daunting, and you might struggle to decide how to start. Thankfully, in "Let's Travel the World. A Travel Guide and Tips for the 21st Century," my friend Nikki Page has a road map for you. Nikki has written an excellent guide for you to get out there and travel. If you are embarking on your first self-planned trip, you will find all the steps necessary to plan your adventure. If you are a more experienced traveler, you will discover insights and lessons learned from a seasoned traveler. Nikki offers tips for making the most of your travel dollars and how to navigate the hurdles of today's travel landscape. Her tips and thoughtful stories will allow you to learn from her experience and be inspired to take the leap with your own travels.

My hope is that everyone will have the opportunity to travel and explore the world, and with the help of this book you can turn your travel dreams into reality.

Cindy Coan
  Author/Travel Coach
  Slow Travel, How to Travel Long Term.

GET OFF THE COUCH AND ON THE PLANE

*H*ave you ever wanted to just get on a plane and see something new? It's a big world out there and there is so much to see. If you are new to travel or haven't been to a foreign country in a while, I have put together the perfect "how-to" guide for you. This quick read is packed full of useful information that will increase your confidence in traveling, save you money, and protect you from common pitfalls that many travelers find themselves in.

I could tell you what it's like to stand atop Mayan ruins in Belize and imagine the ancient civilization that once inhabited the land, or the feeling of walking the Royal Mile to Edinburgh Castle in Scotland, but wouldn't it be better for you to experience them for yourself? Thanks to my travels, I have broadened my world view and I will never see the world the same again.

But what about the risks? Sure; traveling has risks, but I assure you the payoff is worth it. And like most activities, educating yourself can minimize the risk and maximize the experience. Congratulations; you chose to read this book and in turn, you will get the necessary information to get the most out of your explorations. When you finish you will be able to make the arrangements and follow the practices to ensure a successful trip.

In this book you will learn what it is like to travel in the post COVID modern world. In 2001 the travel world came to a standstill with the 9/11 terrorist attacks. The result was increased security and additional screening processes. Fast forward to 2020 and the industry found itself at a loss again with the outbreak of COVID-19. That global pandemic changed the face of travel once again. Both of these incidents affected millions of travelers, some of whom were devastatingly unprepared. I know what it is like to be trapped outside my own country due to a global pandemic and I learned valuable lessons in the process.

Don't be scared to travel internationally, an estimated 12 million people do it safely every day. The key is to take precautions to minimize the effects when things don't go as planned. This book provides advice and information that can keep you safe and help you mitigate difficult situations should they arise.

I have spent thousands of days abroad and visited several countries. My experiences as an expat and travel enthusiast have yielded an education on world travel that I am excited to share with my readers. Don't miss your opportunity to equip yourself as a globetrotter, put this information into action today!

ARE YOU READY? Let's get started with choosing our destination.

CHOOSING A DESTINATION

*W*here do you dream of going? What do you dream of experiencing?

There are many things to consider when picking your destination. Do you want to sit on a beach and watch the sunset as the tide rolls out for the day, or do you want to walk the Great Wall of China? Both are amazing trips; however, they are very different.

How adventurous are you? Do you want to go to Pamplona Spain to run with the bulls? Or visit one of the many nudist beaches along the Mediterranean? If that's not up your alley maybe a European trip full of history and art through the centuries at the Louvre or seeing Michelangelo's statue of David at the Galleria dell'Accademia in Florence Italy would stir your spirit.

Can you speak and/or read the local languages? Are you able to read signs and ask for directions or help should you need it? For example, if we went to Asia their alphabet is nothing like the United States. What will the sign for our hotel read let alone a sign for a hospital?

What time of year do you want to travel? What's the climate like? London in December is wet and cold, and you might even see snow. In contrast, visiting the city of dreams in the summertime with warmer temperatures offers a much different experience from other seasonal activities.

What do you want to do during your holiday? Are there any events in the area during your time of travel? Is there a music festival or an airshow? Events can also increase accommodation prices and even sell out Airbnb and hotel rooms years in advance.

There's a reason why off-season travel is cheaper. It is generally not the best the country has to offer. However, off-season travel can also provide rare opportunities. You may get a more personal experience with more attention from your hosts and staff.

What about currency? Do you need to make a trip to the bank before you leave? Do you understand how money is going to work? What will your ATM and transaction fees on your credit and debit cards look like? Using a currency calculator on your phone can be helpful; however, understanding the country's money is key to making sure you are not a target of being overcharged or taken advantage of. Take the extra step to ensure you know at least estimated conversion rates.

WHERE SHOULD WE GO?

For the sake of this book, let's go to the next place on my bucket list. I have always dreamed of dancing barefoot on the cobblestone streets of Italy. I imagine the rain falling on me as I dance while breathing in the fresh autumn air. This is just one of the things I want to do on my trip to Europe. Running with the bulls is not for this traveler but visiting the colosseum where brutal history was made is high on the bucket list.

WATCH out Rome here we come!

TRAVEL DOCUMENTS AND VISAS

PASSPORT

*D*o you have a passport? If so, now is a great time to check when it expires. Almost all airlines and many countries require that your passport is valid for at least six months beyond the travel dates. If you don't have a passport, now is the time to get one and it's not that difficult.

An appointment at your local passport acceptance facility is the easiest way to get a passport. Depending on your location, these facilities can be part of a post office, library, or even the courthouse. You can also complete the forms and send the information to the National Passport Processing Center yourself.

However, I have always found it reassuring to go into the passport office to have them overlook the papers to make sure they are all filled out correctly. You will need to provide a picture (NO hats or glasses, and you might even be told not to smile), which these offices can take for you. Having the passport office take your picture avoids the chance of the photo not meeting the criteria for any reason. It's also helpful to have the office mail your passport application. I've been told this can help speed up the process and makes tracking the document easier since it is through their internal system.

Make sure to leave enough time before your travel dates for your visa and passports to be processed. At the time of writing this book, the U.S. Department of State website reports processing can take 6-9 weeks. Recently, it took my friend almost 18 weeks to receive her passport; luckily it showed up less than a week before her trip to Mexico. Like most things, you can pay more to have the application process expedited, but remember, you are dealing with a government agency. There is a fee for the expedited request, and there is no guarantee of how much faster you will receive it.

Tip: Your application will need to include an original birth certificate with a raised seal. The copies supplied by the hospital won't work. In most states, you can order an "original" copy of the document online. In Colorado, we were able to walk into the state building and have one printed for each of our family members except for our oldest. Since she was born in Virginia, we had to order a birth certificate from the state of her birth. The process of requesting her out-of-state birth certificate added an extra four weeks before we could even apply for her passport.

The current cost of applying for a U.S. Passport:

Birth Certificate - $20.00

Passport Fees - $130.00

Shipping fee - $35.00

DRIVER'S LICENSE AND ID

If you are flying domestically, you don't need a passport. You only need a driver's license or state-issued ID to board the aircraft. After the 9/11 attacks, as part of the fight against terrorism, Homeland Security implemented REAL IDs. "It was aimed at eliminating airline terrorism by increasing requirements to obtain documents granting access to domestic planes" (Rodriguez). Basically, you have to provide more paperwork to receive one of these government IDs. REAL IDs will eventually become a requirement.

Almost two decades later, the government pushed out the deadline for airlines to require REAL IDs from October 1, 2020, to May 7, 2025. When REAL IDs finally go into effect your license or state-issued ID must have a star in a black circle or a yellow star in the top right corner.

Since Italy is an international destination, we will need to be traveling with our passports. Even though I don't drive in most countries, I always take my driver's license. You never know when you might need it and it also works as a second form of Identification.

Tip: If you have an Apple Wallet you can speed up your check-in process and protect your identity by using Digital IDs. TSA is using this new technology for a "faster, easier travel experience". For domestic flights, your Digital ID can be used in place of your physical ID and boarding passes.

"Add an eligible driver's license or state ID to the Apple Wallet app. Present your ID at select TSA checkpoints by tapping your iPhone or Apple Watch" (Digital).

VACCINATIONS AND PILLS

Do you have your shots and medications? Vaccinations and medications are nothing new. People have been getting shots and taking pills to travel for decades. Prescriptions for Malaria, shots for yellow fever, hepatitis A & B, Cholera... the list goes on. The latest one to hit this list was the COVID vaccine. Many countries, like the United States, are still requiring non-citizen travelers to be fully vaccinated to enter (Requirement).

This is something that you must ask yourself as a traveler, what are you willing to put into your body? Most countries recommend a number of vaccines before visiting; however, some countries require certain vaccinations before entering. Your local health department should be able to provide you with a list of required and recommended vaccines and medications based on your travel locations. Check with your primary physician, if they cannot provide what's needed, you can make an appointment at a travel clinic or health department. Some vaccines require weeks to be effective, and in some cases a booster dose may be required. Make sure to leave enough time between the vaccination and your travel.

Today a quick search shows we don't have to be vaccinated or tested for Covid if we are traveling from the United States to Italy. There is also no required quarantine time. Unlike my last trip when my family was required to test before we could enter our home country's borders, this time I don't have to be tested or be vaccinated to return home. As I said, people who are not citizens are still required to be, fully vaccinated when entering the U.S. Keep in mind, entry requirements are subject to change at any time.

Visas and Onward Travel

What is onward travel, and do we need it? Since I'm coming from the United States and hold a U.S. passport, most countries will apply a tourist visa stamp to the passport pages. We will receive our visa stamp upon arrival. If our visit is for business or other purposes, the application for the specific visa will need to be applied for weeks or months prior to our trip. Even if you are visiting solely for tourism, some countries do require additional paperwork to be submitted prior to travel. Many countries like Panama require you to show proof of how you are leaving the country. This is where onward travel becomes part of the paperwork to either board the flight or enter the country.

It's pretty simple to meet the onward travel requirements. You need to see how long the country says the visa is good for and make sure to book a flight out of the country before your number of days is up. The majority of the time your roundtrip ticket will suffice. The issue arises when you travel one way with an open-ended return date. If you are not sure how long you will be staying, I recommend purchasing a ticket that allows changes to your travel dates without additional fees.

Most of the time the airlines will ask for onward travel when checking in; however, any immigration officer can ask for this paperwork. Not all countries require a flight out, some will allow bus or train tickets to be used. Once again, every country is different so make sure you understand what documentation is required before travel is booked.

A quick search shows I can stay in Italy for 90 days with my U.S. passport. Italy requires passports must be valid for at least three months from travel to enter the country; however, another search shows the airline requirements are different. According to United Airlines, there must be at least six months after our return date to board the flight to Rome. It doesn't matter what the country's rules are if you can't board the flight to get there. This nomad will ensure she has at least a year because you never know where I will go next. Although you may be able to update a passport internationally, it's going to cost more and take time out of your travels. In most cases, you will need to schedule an appointment at the embassy.

PAPERWORK FOR CLEARING IMMIGRATION

I have always had to present my passport to Immigration, but onward travel can sometimes be displayed on my phone. I recommend traveling with printed copies just in case your battery dies, or authorities ask for a paper copy. If you have a round-trip ticket, many times onward travel doesn't even have to be pulled out when checking in for a flight since it's already in their system. However, you still might have to prove onward travel when going through immigration. I keep all my travel documents together with my passport. This makes it easy to show the airline staff and security officers any documentation they may need. Do not hand all your documentation to the officer, only give them what they ask for. I usually take a photo of all travel documents on my phone and upload it to the cloud just in case the papers go missing. Memorize your password just in case you are unable to access your phone or laptop. If there's a problem, you will still be able to access your documents from another device.

Tips:

Always keep a photocopy of your passport. This way you can leave the original in the locked hotel safe while sightseeing. Aside from entering and leaving the country, it is uncommon for you to need your actual passport. Be sure the photocopy includes the photo page. I bring the printed copy with me, so I don't have to locate a printer, which proved to be a challenge in Mexico on one of my visits. I will take a photo of the visa stamp when I arrive. If my hotel offers a printer, I will then add a printed copy containing the visa stamp. This will be done so I have documentation of who I am and the visa if my phone happens to be stolen or runs out of battery.

Research the location of your country's embassy and have it with you during your travels. If you encounter problems with losing documents or legal issues or just need help, the embassy is your lifeline.

The https://travel.state.gov/ site will have all the

rules and requirements for the countries you are consid-
ering traveling to. The website lists all requirements such
as vaccination, testing, and which visas are needed.

Register with the embassy through the Smart Trav-
eler Enrollment Program (Smart). This free program has
a lot of benefits. Most importantly, it is how the U.S.
Embassy can reach you during an emergency. Be it a
natural disaster or a family emergency, being able to get
in contact is essential.

2020 taught us the whole world can change in a second. Staying informed and aware of what's happening is key to safe travels. These two resources were essential for information when my family's fear of not being able to come back to our home country became our reality during the 2020 lockdown in Costa Rica. You can read more about what lockdown in Costa Rica looked like in my last book, "228 Days Trapped in Paradise: The Diary of an Expat Chica in Costa Rica".

IS THAT TICKET REALLY THE CHEAPEST

My goals are to take a tour of the Vatican in Rome and also do some high-end shopping in Milan, the fashion capital of the world. In addition, I would like to ride on the high-speed trains that are popular in Europe. Fortunately, the cheapest flights to Italy happen to land in Florence which is between both cities. Florence also has a train station with routes to both Rome and Milan for around $20-$60 each way. I will have to be sure to factor those transportation costs into my trip budget.

Let's book some airline tickets. I'm flying out of Denver CO (DIA) to Florence, Italy (FCO). A quick search on a third-party site like skyscanner.com or kayak.com will show you the most common flights.

This will allow you to see what airlines are flying to and from the destination. This step is important in helping us find the best fair.

I want to fly out a couple of days before any tours so I will be over the jet lag and get familiar with the area. Going straight to the airline site, it looks like Delta has a flight; while United uses a Star Alliance partner, Lufthansa on the 2nd leg of the trip. This is important to note because the bag and weight allowance can change depending on the airline.

To clarify, you might book the tickets through Expedia with the first leg on a United flight and the second leg on British Airways. United is part of the Star Alliance and British Airways is part of the Oneworld Alliance. An "Alliance" is a global network of airlines. Since the airlines are in separate alliances, they do not have to follow the same baggage requirements. British Airways might include a free bag while United might charge for the bag or they might not charge for the bag, but weight and size limits could be a problem.

The third-party site shows the cheapest option with round-trip tickets in Economy seating for $1,254. Booking straight through United, an economy plus seat is priced at $1,552. The Delta flight is priced at $1,863. Depending on the aircraft size, you may have an additional seating upgrade option before the business and first-class section

3rd Party Booking

Airline	Class	Departure City	Departure Date		Arrival City	Arrival Date	Arrival Time
United Airlines	Economy Plus	Denver **DIA**	9/29/23 12:00 AM		Chicago Ohare **ORD**	9/29/23 0:00	2:34 PM
Lufthansa	Economy Plus	Chicago Ohare **ORD**	9/23/23 12:00 AM		Florence **FCO**	9/30/23 0:00	8:20 AM
Delta	Economy Plus	Florence **FCO**	10/30/23 12:00 AM		New York, Kennedy **JFK**	10/30/23 0:00	5:20 PM
Delta	Economy Plus	New York, Kennedy **JFK**	10/30/23 12:00 AM		Denver **DIA**	10/30/23 0:00	10:20 PM

$1,254

United Airlines

Class	Departure City	Departure		Arrival City	Arrival	Arrival Time
Economy Plus	Denver **DIA**	9/29/23 11:55 AM		Chicago Ohare **ORD**	9/29/23 0:00	2:34 PM
Economy Plus	Chicago Ohare **ORD**	9/23/23 4:10 PM		Florence **FCO**	9/30/23 0:00	8:20 AM
Economy Plus	Florence **FCO**	10/30/23 9:55 AM		New York/Newark **EWR**	10/30/23 0:00	2:55 PM
Economy Plus	New York/Newark **EWR**	10/30/23 6:50 PM		Denver **DIA**	10/30/23 0:00	7:15 PM

| Booking Through United.com | $1,552.00 | | | |
| Booking Through my Credit Card Service | $1,022.00 | | Savings of | $530.00 |

Delta Airlines

Class	Departure City	Departure Date		Arrival City	Arrival Date	Arrival Time
Delta Comfort	Denver **DIA**	9/29/23 12:50 PM		New York, Kennedy **JFK**	9/29/23 0:00	6:07 PM
Delta Comfort	New York, Kennedy **JFK**	9/29/23 7:25 PM		Florence **FCO**	9/30/23 0:00	10:20 AM
Delta Comfort	Florence **FCO**	10/30/23 12:50 PM		New York, Kennedy **JFK**	10/30/23 0:00	5:20 PM
Delta Comfort	New York, Kennedy **JFK**	10/30/23 7:29 PM		Denver **DIA**	10/30/23 0:00	10:20 PM

| Booking Through Delta.com | $1,863.00 | | | |
| Booking Through my Credit Card Service | $1,114.00 | | Savings of | $749.00 |

THE THINGS I LOOK FOR WHEN BUYING TICKETS

There are several things to consider when shopping for the best airline tickets. It's a simple situation of you get what you pay for. The cheapest tickets offer the bare minimum. It is a seat on a plane with the minimal amount of room and options.

For this example, I will use the United economy plus and the Delta comfort fare. These seats are equal to the seat that I would be getting on the third-party site. It is in the economy section with the standard upgrades of no change fees.

HERE IS WHERE THE DIFFERENCE COMES IN

BAGS

Do you want to add bags to the cheaper tickets? If so, it's going to cost you. The upgraded seats on Delta and United allow us one checked bag, a carry-on, and a personal bag. On the cheaper tickets, our luggage is not included. They only allow us one small personal bag. The size of this personal bag is smaller than my backpack, meaning every bag I bring is going to cost me.

REFUNDABLE

Is the flight refundable? This is often where you will find one of the largest differences in the price of tickets. The cheapest tickets often do not offer a refund option or allow changes. It is very common for things not to go as planned. I have had to change my travel plans enough times to know the cost of unchangeable tickets.

What if something happens and you are not able to travel? On both United and Delta, the ticket I've chosen is refundable or changeable. The third-party site is not refundable, even though they are using some of the same flights and I get to pick from the same seats. Are you willing to walk away from the money you spent on the ticket? Do the cheaper flights offer a refundable option? If so, how much is it going to cost to add the refundable option?

LAYOVERS

How many layovers are there and how long are they? Traveling takes energy and is hard on the body. The longer the travel, the more jet lag you may experience. Keep in mind this not only adds travel time but also adds to travel expenses in lodging or sleeping in an airport. In addition, you will need to factor in meals, and airport food is not cheap.

Another consideration is where the layovers occur. A domestic layover is less of an issue than an international one. For domestic flights, you usually do not need to go through security before boarding your next flight unless you leave the terminal. Immigration and customs inspections are other potential issues if you are traveling through multiple countries. Familiarity with the airport and the distance between the gates should be taken into consideration. You should take time to look up a map of the airport and locate your terminals, gates, security points, access to food, and any other services you may need.

I will keep in mind Chicago O'Hare (ORD) is a big airport; I have had to run it many times. Inevitably, the gate where I land is on the opposite end of the airport from the international terminal. Make sure you leave enough time to go through the process. It sucks missing a flight, especially the last redeye out. This is another reason to have insurance on your ticket.

Both the outgoing and return on United have only about an hour and a half layover. Can we make it to our connecting flight in this amount of time?

Remember, you board flights 30-50 minutes before taking off. Since I don't have to go through customs or immigration until the second flight and I'm not traveling with young kids, I should be able to make the outgoing flight.

If there was an immigration or customs checkpoint during the layover this would be a different story and has me doubting the return flight on United that lands in Newark (EWR). As a rule, I try to allow an hour or two between domestic flights; and two to three hours when going through customs and immigration checkpoints. This extra time helps keep us from feeling rushed and gives us time to visit the restroom and stretch our legs during the connection.

I have gone through these checkpoints in record times like fifteen minutes. However, the same checkpoint has also taken me over two hours to get through. On the other hand, we don't want to sit around the airport for six to twelve hours on a long layover. If you do have to hang out at an airport for long amounts of time, I recommend checking to see if there's anything to see. The Cultural Experience Zone in Incheon International Airport (ICN) is where travelers can see live music and dance performances; as well as learn how to make crafts (Incheon). The rain vortex in Changi Airport (SIN) is on my list to see. Sure, it won't take hours to see a waterfall, but it will kill some time (Changi).

ADJUSTED PRICE

Once I added the extra cost of bags and the refundable option to the cheaper $1,254 third-party ticket, the new total was $1,883. The add-ons make the "cheaper" ticket the most expensive in the end.

I can still save more money by using the booking service offered by my credit card. This is different from booking with points. Many credit cards offer services to book travel reservations for flights, lodging, and car rentals. Some cards even offer tour booking as well. This is just a booking service. When it comes time to pay, you do not have to use your miles and some allow other forms of payment (not the card offering the service). Check with your credit card company to see what services they provide.

If I book the same United flight using the travel booking service offered by my credit card, the flight will cost me $1,022, a savings of $530 from the original price. Through my credit card company, the Delta flight is listed at $1,114, meaning if I book through the credit card website, I will save $749. On top of this, my tickets will have good travel insurance automatically included when I book using this service.

In the end, the cheapest fight is really not the cheapest. Today the cheapest flight would be on United Airlines, but this flight is a little short on the return travel time, making me a little leery of not having enough time at the customs and immigration checkpoints. Once again, I have flown internationally with both airlines and had good experiences. Since the Delta flight departure times will work better and allows me more time between flights, I might just pay the extra $92 for convenience and the peace of mind.

Do your research. This time it is cheaper for me to book through the credit card service, but next time I might find a better deal through a different option. On separate occasions, I have found the most affordable option through each of the other methods mentioned.

Tips:

If you are not seeing a great deal, try clearing the cache of your device and deleting cookies before re-running your next search.

Southwest Airlines offers two free bags. Keep this in mind when comparing flight prices. Unfortunately, they were not an option for our example destination.

MY FIRST FREE AIRLINE TICKET

Who doesn't want to travel for free? Talk about an exciting chapter to write; however, it was a little hard trying to pick out what adventure I should share, with so many stories about me flying and traveling for cheap or free.

Why not go back to where it all began? I was a 13-year-old girl on my way home from a summer class trip to Washington D.C. It was my second time in the air, my first time had been five days before when our flight left Colorado.

To say this girl got a taste for travel is an understatement. That school trip changed my life. The monuments, the Tomb of the Unknown Soldier, and the International Spy Museum were so educational. Looking back on this experience I learned more during the five days on that trip than I had all year at school.

We were all sitting on the flight waiting to take off, when the pilot came over the intercom system and informed us the plane was too heavy for take-off. The ground crew had dumped as much fuel as they could, but it was still not enough weight. He went on to inform us that we couldn't take off until five people volunteered to get off the flight.

GET ME OFF THIS PLANE

I was scared of flying to begin with. All I had heard was the plane is too heavy, the ground crew just dumped fuel and it was still not safe to take off! The scene kept flashing before my eyes of the plane running out of fuel halfway through the flight, crashing to the earth, and leading me to an awful demise.

One of the teachers said she was willing to take four kids with her on the next flight. Mine was the first hand in the air saying they could have my seat. I just wanted off the plane that had less fuel than it had 10 minutes earlier, nothing else mattered.

Now over the years of travel, many of my flights have experienced this problem and I've learned it's nothing to worry about. People give up seats, they dump extra fuel, and with the lighter load off you go.

LIFE-CHANGING

This moment ended up being life-changing for me. After we deboarded the aircraft, the lady behind the counter handed me my voucher. Right then it hit me. All I heard were frightening things, I didn't hear what the pilot was saying. The airline was offering free flights and food vouchers for seats.

These five people would be booked on the next flight at no additional charge. They would also receive a $20 food voucher that allowed them to eat in the airport during their wait. As a bonus for the inconvenience, each delayed traveler would receive a $320 flight voucher to use towards another flight.

What had just happened? Not only would I eat dinner for free at the airport restaurant, but I was also going to fly free on my next trip. All in exchange for my time and seat!

FOOD & FLIGHT VOUCHERS

Later that summer our parents used the vouchers to send me and my ten-year-old sister on our first unac-companied minor flight. The $320 voucher was enough money for two round-trip tickets from Denver Colorado (DIA) to Portland Oregon International Airport (PDX), plus an airport dinner with a soda. During our travel, we were able to camp on the beach with our cousins. It was another amazing trip! At that moment I was hooked, I wanted to travel, especially if it was for free.

Nikki Page, you are never too young to start tasting the world.

TRAVEL FOR CHEAP WITH MILES

$\mathcal{A}$re you using your miles? If not, why not?

Oh my, how I love my miles! I was able to use my miles to fly on a Delta flight from Liberia Costa Rica (LIR) to Denver Colorado International (DIA) for $82.08. The total price of the flight included taxes and exit fees.

This is how it worked.

The original ticket was $319.83 or 31,983 Miles. I had 23,775 miles from my Capital One Credit Card that I had been saving up over time. I was living in Costa Rica at the time and my objective was to find a free flight or at least a cheap one. This was the only way I could travel back to see my family.

CHECK FLIGHTS DAILY

My husband calls it an obsession, I call it saving money so we can travel more often. When I know there's an upcoming trip or a country that I want to see, I start watching flights. Some of these flights are 12 months out. When you are looking for killer deals, it may take extra time.

On this occasion, we had been living in Central America for a little over a year and I was extremely homesick. At that time, an average flight from Costa Rica to Denver was between $250 - $425 depending on how far in advance you booked. A summer trip had not been planned for in the budget; however, I had been saving my miles.

Every morning with my cup of coffee, this "travel girl" would check her credit card miles and flight prices. Sometimes the airlines will throw tickets on sale if they add another flight, just so they can start to fill up the plane. Other times the ticket might be the last seat.

I logged into my miles account and watched tickets for months, praying they would go on sale. Using the credit card site, I could buy my tickets using both my miles or just pay with the card. I also would check directly on the airline websites: United,

Delta, and Southwest since they all had regular routes. Like I said before, sometimes these prices are better than booking straight through the credit card site.

Depending on what card I'm using, I'm able to book tickets through the airline using the credit card and then redeem the miles to pay the amount of the ticket. This is a nice advantage when the airlines announce sales because you are still able to use your credit card miles for the ticket. One day there it was, the golden ticket as I called it. Since I had a valid passport and miles, all it took was hitting the book now button. I simply had to arrive at the airport in 74 hours.

At the time the plane ticket and fees were $319.83. The miles on the credit card were worth $237.75 so my final ticket price ended up being a remaining balance of $82.08, including all taxes and fees.

I don't know about you but to me, that's an amazing deal.

So next time you're swiping a credit card, stop and ask yourself if you are using their miles program.

Tip: Make sure your exit taxes are on your ticket. Not all airlines add the tax, but I guarantee you are going to pay it before you leave. Not all countries will take a credit card at the airport. Some require cash at the exit point. If the tax is not included on your ticket, make sure you are prepared with the proper form of payment.

SECRETS TO GETTING FREE AIRLINE TICKETS

*I*t's no secret free airline tickets are one of my favorite things. They can be hard to get your hands on. These offers don't come around every day and are limited amounts, usually on a first come first serve basis. Do you want to know one of my top secrets to get some sweet deals? It's called LISTENING! This word was a game-changer for me when it comes to getting free travel.

Flights get canceled all the time for many reasons like weather, overbooking, mechanical problems, and even pilots not showing up. These issues can be frustrating, making travel times longer than you had planned. They also create problems for the airline personnel who must shuffle passengers around while trying to get everyone safely to their destinations.

When cancellations like this happen, the airlines try to find ways to accommodate more people on flights. If there are no additional seats left on the plane, they often ask other passengers to give up their seats. The airlines entice travelers to help keep those whose flights were canceled happy. They entice travelers with vouchers for free food, hotels, flights, and sometimes even first-class upgrades to those willing to take a later flight.

WHAT'S YOUR TIME WORTH

What is your time worth on this trip? This is a question I ask myself right before my travels. If I can't afford to be late to my destination it doesn't matter what the offer is for my time. However, if I have some flexibility with my time and travels why not take advantage of free travel offers and upgrades?

LISTENING!

As soon as I walk into the airport I start listening. When an airline needs people to give up seats, they will most likely start announcing it over the intercom. This announcement can happen at any time. You want to make sure you're prepared to find the first ticket counter so you can grab the free ticket and travel vouchers before they are all gone.

Most people are on their mobile devices with headphones in. These people are not listening, so we want to use this to our advantage. You now have a better chance of being first in line when an offer is announced.

Tips:

When you check in, ask how full the flight is. If the plane is full or overbooked, I ask if they are offering flight vouchers for people to give up seats. It never hurts to ask!

The staging area is where people hang out until they start boarding the aircraft. Sit close enough to be first. I recommend sitting as close to the ticket counter as you can.

When you hear an announcement about needing people to give their seats up. Head straight to where they tell you to go. Most of the time it's the ticket counter that's right next to where I'm sitting.

Make sure to LISTEN; yes, I said it again. They might tell you to go somewhere other than the ticket counter such as a specific gate or customer service. You don't want to miss out on the deal because you were not paying attention and went to the wrong place!

DON'T BE AFRAID TO ASK QUESTIONS

I have 7 questions I ask.

Question #1 - How much is the voucher worth?

I have received vouchers from $23 to $750 that I could apply to things such as food, lodging, transportation, upgrades, and even first-class airline tickets.

Question #2 - What time is the new flight?

Question #3 - What class are they putting me in on the next flight?

This is important if your old ticket has an upgrade on the seat. We don't want a downgrade on the next flight, you want just the opposite. Can we say FREE upgrade or more money on the travel voucher?

Sometimes just asking if the seats are going to be upgraded is all it takes to go from coach to First-Class at no charge. I found this out on a trip coming back from Florida. My husband Steve and I had just given up our seats. By simply taking a flight one hour later, we each received a $500 flight voucher.

As we stood at the counter waiting for the lady to give us our new tickets and vouchers, Steve asked if the seats were going to be first-class. The woman working the counter smiled at him as she typed a little more on her computer. She then gave him a big smile and said, "Why yes Mr. Page I do have a couple of first-class tickets available, would you like them?" Remember to ask, if you don't you might miss out.

Question #4 - Are they offering food vouchers?

You're going to be waiting around and probably going to get hungry. Remember airport food can be expensive adding to your travel cost. Many airlines will give you food vouchers if you ask.

Question #5 – Are they offering accommodations?

If the next flight is not until the following day, you want to make sure they're offering food and sleep accommodations. Nine out of ten times they do. If not, you must ask yourself, how much are food and lodging going to cost? Sometimes a hotel and extra food are not in the budget. Is the flight voucher worth the extra money and time you will have to spend? Is spending the night in an airport worth saving money? People will do crazy things to see the world. Yes, in my younger years, I had spent the night on the airport floor just for a free airline ticket.

Question #6 - How long is the travel voucher valid?

Question #7 - Are there blackout dates? If so, where do I find the dates?

Each airline has its own voucher process. Some automatically add the voucher to your phone's app.

You can see them on your device as you stand at the ticket counter. Other airlines are not so quick. If your voucher is not generated immediately, ask how long it takes for the ticket to show up. Make sure to get a confirmation number and phone number just in case you have to follow up.

Tip: Keep track of all paperwork or links they give you. Taking a picture on your phone of the document is also helpful just in case things go missing.

INSURANCE

*D*o you Need Traveler's Insurance? The answer is YES!

Even when traveling to a country with cheap or affordable healthcare, insurance is a good idea. It only takes a second for a costly accident to happen or for your health issues to catch up to you. I will use Costa Rica as an example since I had major medical care there. This beautiful country has some of the best care I have ever experienced and affordable is an understatement. But without insurance, your treatment options may be limited.

You should check with your normal insurance to find out what they cover and the limitations on your coverage before you travel. It is extremely rare that your insurance will cover care outside the United

States. If it does have international coverage, there are usually restrictions on what is covered. There may be issues with the medical provider accepting your insurance as well. Travelers insurance or an additional binder on your policy are highly advised.

In Costa Rica, the average doctor's office costs about $60-$120 per visit. I had an ultrasound of my whole abdomen for less than $100, that's very affordable care. However, I had a friend who was in a moto wreck and spent three days in the hospital where he had to pay for his treatment upfront. The bills were in the $25K range (a fraction of what it would have been in the states), but since he didn't have access to that kind of money, insurance was a lifesaver. Another friend had to be airlifted after a fall at the swimming pool. A week in the ICU, and surgery on her foot was well over $50K. If you can't afford the extra $40-$150 in insurance, ask yourself how you are going to pay a large medical bill or upfront payment in the thousands if you end up needing emergency care.

Another benefit of most traveler's insurance policies is being able to cancel your trip or change travel dates. This is nice since travel has become unpredictable. If you don't have insurance and a flight is canceled or delayed, are you going to stay in the airport if they don't offer vouchers? Can you afford the hotel or extra days of travel if things require a change? The expense of changes to travel almost always costs more than that of adding insurance. Traveler's insurance often offers additional resources for extended stays including lodging, transportation, and meals.

Most airlines and many credit cards offer insurance on travel. AARP is another option for mature travelers. In all policies the fine print is important, you should read the insurance binder, so you know what your rights are and how to turn in a claim if needed. I have experienced issues adding insurance to a one-way ticket through the airlines. I was told the insurance was only in effect for 24 hours of my travel since there was no end date. My solution was to obtain insurance through my credit card instead.

Avoid adding insult to injury with a trip ruined not only because of a bad turn of events, but also returning with large bills that could have been avoided. Make the investment and arrangements to protect yourself ahead of time so you can have peace of mind as you enjoy your trip of a lifetime.

TRAVELING WITH INFANTS AND CHILDREN

*D*id you know infants fly for free? Most airlines within the U.S. allow infants under the age of two to fly free if they sit on your lap. Many international airlines also have discounted fares and some even offer free travel for infants. Just like adults, babies still need paperwork and passports when traveling internationally.

Often, the strollers and car seats are also free, and they don't count as your bags. Many airlines will also allow you to check the strollers at the gate for no additional charge. I have even been allowed to carry the smaller umbrella style on board since they can fold up small enough to be placed in the overhead bins. The fullness of the flight may be a determining factor as to whether you can carry it on or have to check it. If you check them at the gate, nine-out-of-ten times it's waiting for you as you come off the aircraft upon landing.

I have traveled with children on my lap, it works... However, if you can afford to buy your child their own seat, it's nice to strap the infant carrier or car seat in. For the safety of the child, the FAA encourages you to do so (Flying). Always check with the car seat manufacturers and the airline to ensure they are approved for your air travel.

We have trained our kids to sit in these seats for long periods during car travel. The same mindset goes when sitting on an aircraft, we need to sit in our seats and be strapped in just like in an automobile. You never know when you are going to hit turbulence. Bringing the car seat on an aircraft also keeps it from not being thrown around with the checked bags.

If your child uses a booster seat, you should look into the CARES device as booster seats are not allowed to be used during takeoff and landing. Currently, this is the restraint approved by the FAA. This is a cargo strap system to restrain your child. It is a four-point system that looks like they're strapped into a racecar. Should the plane hit some unexpected turbulence, or an emergency happens, the harness will keep your child safely in their seat.

It's always good to have a breast, bottle, or pacifier

ready for the baby. The sucking helps them pop their ears during pressure changes. For me, I always have gum ready. There's nothing like having ear pressure during take-off and landing. Don't forget, your baby feels it too.

When traveling with kids I usually pack gummies to help with their ears and small treats for snacks. Many little games, puzzles, and coloring books will be pulled out of the bag during the trip. A lot of kids' movies will be downloaded. For me, this is not a time to be concerned about screen time. It keeps them quiet during travel. Especially on long flights, the movie or game helps to break up the time while also making travel fun for kids.

To achieve greatness, we practice and take every opportunity to teach. They are never too young to start traveling. We have four children and all of them started air travel at a young age. So, what does greatness look like when it comes to traveling with four children? If you ask me, it's all about surviving the trip.

Yep, I was the crazy mom going through the airport like a drill sergeant. The one-year-old was strapped in a double stroller. The stubborn three-year-old refused to let me push him as he proudly wheeled his little Spiderman carry-on in front of his five and six-year-old sisters. Each child was responsible for their bag. They were packed with little treasures that would be pulled out during the flight. We walked one at a time in single file lines as we loaded and unloaded in and out of the elevators and on and off the "magical stairs".

On the Disney trip, the goal was, "no child left behind". Marching through the airport, they looked like little soldiers. We used numbers and did roll calls. It sounds crazy, but it worked; trying to wrangle four kids through an airport can be hard. I can still hear the words today, "Count off." I was always number one and dad was always number six. Somewhere in between these numbers, I should hear four little voices. They would line up and count off every time we had to go through a security point or bathroom break.

I took every opportunity to teach. We located our destination on maps before the adventure had even begun. We practiced how to get through the airport weeks before we even started our travels. Each child had a job to help us get to our destination. They were responsible for something like reading signs, finding ticket counters, and security checkpoints. We even studied what aircraft we were flying on.

Sure, it took some extra time and a lot of work as a mom. They packed their bags and learned new skills. It proved to be worth all the extra work as I listened to my son years later carrying on a conversation with an engineer from NASA during one of our boardings. This mom was in awe as my son talked about the aircraft we were boarding. He had researched the plane, something I had not even done on this particular trip.

One thing is for sure, as a mom, I achieved greatness on this adventure. No child was lost or misplaced during our travels.

TRAVELING WITH A WHEELCHAIR

Steve is always giving me a hard time about being at the airport too early. The first flight I ever missed was because my sister and I were not prepared when we traveled with my disabled mother. She is non-ambulatory so she needs a lot of assistance. I think this trip was a defining part of the way I travel and why I feel the need to be so early.

The goal was to get our mom to the family reunion in Kansas City. Two young sisters, each of us with a baby in our arms and our disabled mom in her wheelchair took on air travel. This whole trip would have been different if mom could have brought her electric scooter on the flight.

Numerous airlines don't charge to check assistance devices like canes, walkers, wheelchairs, and even electric scooters. Most of the time you can check them at either the ticket counter or the gate. So, what was the problem and why did mom have to go in the push wheelchair?

The first problem was that her wheels used lithium-ion batteries that had to be removed and placed in a carry-on. This is not easy to do, but we girls were up for the challenge, and I know it could be done. We had to disassemble and place the batteries in a bag at the gate. What's one more bag?

The second problem was trying to find a rental van after we landed that had a lift to transport the scooter. It could be done, but it was going to cost a pretty penny, and the van had to be reserved months in advance. Whether or not we like it, money plays a big role in the way we travel. Handicapped rooms, cars, and accommodations can cost more.

With all of that aside, mom still could not take her wheels. In the end, the scooter was too heavy to be placed on the aircraft. Fortunately, we were aware of this before we even left for the airport and made other plans. What I was not prepared for was the extra time it would take to get through the parking lot pushing my disabled mother with the babies and luggage.

Arriving two hours before the flight is what's recommended. We were only running about fifteen minutes late after the parking lot fiasco. This is where the running shoes come in. I hate running through the airport, but when you are late that's what you do. But this is not the case when you are traveling with people who need assistance to get on the flight.

Traveling with my disabled father is much easier. Dad needs wheelchair assistance to get through the airport, but he can still walk down the aisle of the aircraft without the assistance of a chair. Since mom can't walk at all, she has to be placed in a special chair to get her down the narrow rows and this requires her to be loaded on the flight during priority boarding. The extra time it was going to take to get her through security and into the special chair was just enough to make us miss our flight. Yes, a 15-minute delay can make a big difference in travel especially when it comes to being allowed to board a flight.

Now here's the cool part about traveling in a wheelchair. It can be easy if you know what you are doing, and even easier if you ask for assistance. Mom was a special case and having babies with us added even more of a challenge. I now book wheelchair assistance when booking flights for my parents. The airline website or app should ask if additional assistance is needed and what type.

This way the airline knows we are traveling with handicapped or elderly people, and they are prepared with the staff to assist them. I can pull right up in the drop-off lane at the airport, and they will bring the wheelchair right out to the car. Someone from the airline will push the passenger and their bags through security and right to the gate.

This saves time in the security lines. Most of the time they allow the whole family to go through the shorter lines and even do the early boarding. When traveling internationally with my dad I have even been able to skip the long immigration and customs lines and allowed to walk through the short priority line checkpoints. The cool part is, I don't need to worry about my stepmom getting lost in the airport when she flies alone since they take her right from my car to her gate.

It gives me peace of mind to have people help transport my parents. My dad can walk with a cane and my stepmom doesn't usually use a wheelchair, but neither would be able to walk the whole airport. These services and the extra help have allowed my parents to travel well into their older years.

As far as mom is concerned, she proved she could still travel on airplanes without being able to walk. Once she proved it could be done, she informed all of us that she would never do it again. Even though it was hard being transferred to the special chair and then to the plane seat, it was doable. As a fellow traveler, it makes me sad to see how hard this trip was on her. Not having her usual devices was more difficult than we anticipated. To this day I believe she would have traveled more if she could bring her electric wheelchair on the aircraft.

Make sure to check with the airline on the requirements when traveling with electric chairs. Each airline has its own weight requirements and many even require the chair to be placed on its side. There are also regulations on the different kinds of batteries and how they have to be stored during transport.

Tip: Check your assistance devices at the gate. Remember to tag any assistant devices even when they are being checked. Since the devices should be loaded and unloaded right at the aircraft there is less likelihood of them being lost if you check them at the gate.

FLYING FREE WITH MILES

$\mathcal{M}$y first free international flight was from Denver International Airport (DIA) in Colorado to Glasgow Airport Scotland (GLA) in business class. Yes, you heard me correctly, FREE international plane ticket with the extra inches.

LET'S TALK ABOUT HOW I DID IT

This "travel girl" wishes she could tell you she saved her points and booked an international trip in a couple of months, but that's not what happened.

I was a young mother of four, who just wanted to travel with her husband on a business trip. Now when I say business trip, you must understand that his company was sending him to places like Scotland,

India, and Italy. He would call talking about all the incredible museums he had just visited or the wine he was drinking after the first-class upgrade. Most of these calls would come as I was changing a dirty diaper or breaking up a sibling fight.

There was no way I could afford the business-class ticket on our budget. Heck, during this time of my life, I couldn't afford the basic upgrade or even the back seat of the flight. The dream of just traveling with him while he worked was enough to find a way and the way was MILES.

The first thing to do is to research the cards out there. Every card has different rewards, points, miles, and cash back. Read the small print on the contracts. Know your blackout days and how to redeem your points and miles.

Many travelers like to use airline credit cards because most include free or cheaper bags, plus upgrades on seats. My Capital One Venture card is the first card I bring with me when traveling. It's not a promo plug, it's just a fact. I am able to accumulate miles faster than any other offers I have received. It is also very easy to redeem the miles or assign my miles to travel purchases.

Remember, every traveler is different so depending on your shopping and credit profile there may be better options for you. Be sure to read the fine print and weigh out which program best suits your needs.

HOW TO FUND YOUR TRIP

It took just over a year for me to save enough miles for our trip. But saving miles wasn't the only approach. I also cut out all the little things like the coffee shop. Yep, you heard me, the first thing to save for travel was putting the designer coffee or whatever your spending vice is on hold and start putting that money in the piggy bank. It's not easy, but you can do it if you really want to see the world.

For some, this may be foregoing the bar for a few drinks at home, or simply cooking meals rather than eating out. Basically, it comes down to changing your habits in everyday life to cut corners and save money. In the end, it comes to priorities. Would you rather have your drinks at the local pub or on the beach? Do you want delivery pizza or woodfired perfection from a little town in Sicily?

Use your money for travel instead of everyday life. Although I don't believe in going into too much debt to travel, I do believe we can justify some travel debt as the cost of education and life experience. Similar to obtaining student loans in order to expand your knowledge. So, a little debt might be justified in the end, but ultimately my goal is to pay the debt off as soon as it is charged.

At the time of my first free international ticket, our best card for earning miles was a Visa. Everything my husband and I bought was put on this credit card. Like I said I don't want debt, but I want the miles that come with charging my purchases so how do we do this without going into debt? The first rule is to make sure to never charge anything you can't pay off right away.

For example, we charged our groceries to our credit card instead of our debit card. Then we would go home and pay off the credit card with a quick transfer from our checking account. I just earned miles while buying food for my family without going into debt. Another way is to pay for your gas with a credit card and then pay it off each month.

To taste the world, the small, cramped seats in the back of the plane are worth it if that's all you can afford. However, if you can afford the upgrade take it. On a long flight, a couple of extra inches makes a big difference.

Steve had a business trip to Scotland on the calendar. It would be his third time walking the Royal Mile without me. I was not going to miss the fourth trip. After saving for months, I had the miles for the ticket, but I'm not sitting in the back of the plane while my husband rides in business class. It took an extra three months of selective spending and saving, plus many hours of watching flights and sales so I could get the upgrade.

I was determined and I studied everything I could about the flights and the cost of tickets with my miles. Since it was our Visa card, I didn't have to book on a particular airline, making our travel options more open. This was key since my husband's ticket was purchased through his employer and I had no control over which airline they chose.

I checked flights every day, sometimes two or three times a day. Watching as the flights would fill up and new ones were added. The miles would increase every time we shopped with the card. Like I said, I wish I could tell you it happened overnight but that was just not the case. To earn enough miles, it took a lot of trips to the store and gas station with cheap coffee made from home.

One day there were enough miles for both the international flight and the upgraded seat from economy to business class. With the tickets obtained, the piggy bank was cracked open revealing how much my habits add up. This mom was going to drink Scotch and tour castles. In addition to the miles earned for the airline ticket, I was now able to upgrade my hotel room and take a couple of tours with the money saved from sacrificing my Starbucks and nights at the bar.

My husband would leave for the office in the morning, leaving me to occupy my time until he returned in the evening. After I came up with enough courage to leave the room alone, the hike to the top of the Royal Mile was done over four times during this trip. It's not an easy walk. I recommend taking your time, even breaking the hike up with a tour of the Catholic Chapel and the graveyard. These are a few of the free sightseeing options I found as a solo day traveler. What can I say, he worked for five days of the ten-day trip and this traveling girl was not going to miss out on anything.

GRAB YOUR BAGS LET'S PACK!

$\mathcal{I}$ know what I'm packing, do you?

The first question is how many bags do you need and how many are you allowed? The upgraded tickets allow us one checked bag, a personal bag, and a carry-on. If you are bouncing around from place to place or taking public transportation, that might be a lot of luggage; however, we are traveling in the fall so we will need warmer clothing. Warm clothing takes up more space than bikinis. Since I booked a 30-day ticket, I will more than likely need to check at least one bag to ensure I take enough warm clothing.

Keep in mind the airlines are more restrictive on bags and charge extra fees during the holidays. Make sure you are packing within the requirements or are prepared to pay the extra fees for oversized or overweight bags, including carry-ons. Even worse is being told you can't travel with your bags because of embargo restrictions limiting the quantity and weight of luggage. During high travel times, the airlines often manage the weight of the plane by reducing the baggage being allowed. It may not matter how much you are willing to pay, sometimes you simply cannot take the items you desire.

PASSPORT CARRIER

Staying organized while traveling is fundamental to making sure not to lose important documents like airline tickets or hotel reservations. I like to use a small purse for quick and easy access to paperwork allowing me to keep all important documents on my body. I make sure to leave enough room in my personal backpack for the small purse/passport carrier so I'm able to place it in the bag if the airline says something about it being an extra bag. Having all my documents together during security and other checkpoints is convenient, reducing the chance of losing them or having something stolen. My husband likes to use more of a wallet carrier that he zips in his cargo pants or the front of his backpack. Fannie packs are making a comeback and work well for travels.

Tip: Always pack a black pen, you are going to need it to fill out your Customs forms. I keep mine with my travel documents for easy access.

HEADPHONES

Headphones are a must. I'm very picky about my headphones. I prefer to listen to an audiobook or watch a show during my travels. The bonus is mine are noise canceling and block out the crying baby or snoring passengers next to me. Silencing your fellow passengers can be the difference between enjoying your travels and being miserable.

My favorite in-ear headphones are Apple AirPods Pro. They are small enough to fit in my personal bag or pocket. The wireless charging case holds over 24 hours of battery, allowing me to charge on the go. Apple AirPods Pros also have noise cancellation, which as I mentioned before is priceless. The light-weight design is great for on the move, but they are not as comfortable long-term as the over-ear style of headphones.

My favorite over-the-ear headphones are the Bose QuietComfort 35 II. They are so comfortable I can wear them for long periods of time. Even with my glasses on they don't hurt my ears or head. They also allow me to change the amount of sound that is allowed in. Once again listening for announcements, especially during the beginning and end of a flight, is important. We're talking about packing; so I ask, how much room? The AirPods take up less room when trying to pack light, but if your plans include listening to an audiobook on the beach or on long train trips, you may want to make the larger version a priority.

CELL PHONE

Truthfully, I don't know anyone who travels without a cell phone nowadays. Before leaving the country, make sure the cell phone is unlocked or that the provider has service in the country you are traveling to. If not, you run the risk of not being able to use it. Even worse, if your photos and documents are stored in the cloud, you might not be able to access your information like reservations, phone numbers, or photos of important travel documents. As a result, you would face missed reservations and confusion when entering the country.

Know how much your international service is going to cost. There's nothing like coming back to an extremely high cell phone bill due to roaming charges and foreign service fees. Some countries have free internet nearly everywhere. You can buy cheap minutes for your cell phones for local calls to taxis, hotels, etc., and use WIFI for your apps. In Costa Rica, it was cheaper for me to spend $10 on a chip that was loaded with a small portion of minutes and use the free internet to communicate with people in the U.S. than the $10/day international calling plan through my U.S. provider.

Be sure to research your options and know the specific settings of your phone for the countries you are visiting before you leave. It is very difficult to find the answers you need once the service does not work. Often it is a simple matter of inputting the necessary credentials in the settings menu of your device. Speak to your provider about how to get the best experience from your device while abroad.

Today's cell phones even work as cameras. Some amazing photos have been taken on my Apple iPhone. The camera is an added bonus when it comes to traveling lightly. Bigger cameras can be nice, but they take up room. I rarely have my large Canon DSLR at the ready when those magic moments happen. On the other hand, my phone is rarely out of reach.

PERSONAL BAG

I like to use my backpack as a personal bag. All the things I will need during the flight will go in this bag. The backpack will be placed under the seat in front of me. My bag has a lot of compartments so I can separate things out. The backpack has a computer compartment that is relatively easy to access while providing protection. I try to keep my other electronics in the outside pockets since they will need to be pulled out at security. The same strategy applies to my liquids, they go in a side pocket for easy access.

Eye masks and earplugs are the next priorities for my personal bag. Travel is bright and loud. On a long 14.5-hour red-eye flight, sleep needs to happen. Before we even get to this part of the trip we will have already been traveling for hours. The flight attendants should turn off the overhead lights for a while, but that does not mean it will be dark. If you are like me, even a little light can keep me from drifting off. Blocking out the person who is on a tablet, using a reading light, or TV can be a challenge making it hard to sleep. This is where the eye mask can be a lifesaver.

We have discussed the bliss of being able to block out unwanted sounds from the plane and other passengers. My headphones do a great job of blocking out these noises; but they also must recharge, hence the earplugs. I prefer the wax style that molds to your ear for swimming over the foam. For long flights, your ears might appreciate the comfort of earplugs over headphones.

. . .

TRAVEL PILLOW

Sleeping or even simply resting your head can be a challenge while strapped upright in an aircraft. A pillow can save you the pain in the neck from the weight of your head as it flops from side to side. Travel pillows are small and fit around your neck making travel more comfortable. This simple solution supports your neck as your head rests gently on memory foam, beans, or gel, depending on the model you prefer. As a bonus, most travel pillows easily snap to your luggage allowing you to strap them to the outside of the bag. This feature leaves space for other important items inside your carry-on.

Computer or Tablet

I can access what I need from my phone; however, I make my living from my computer. It's a no-brainer that 99% of the time it comes with me. Even if my travels don't include work, the laptop is usually taken. I find it easier to research and access my email compared to my phone. The only exception is if there is not going to be a safe in my room. If I am not able to lock up my computer, it might get left behind.

If I plan on doing any book reading, I will most likely take my tablet. It doesn't take up a lot of room so most of the time it gets thrown in at the last minute. I also make sure to download games and movies to the tablet before traveling. These items also pair nicely with headphones for distraction-free viewing.

If I have extra room a physical book always makes it in my personal bag. I read or listen to audibles more than I watch movies or play games, so making sure to have a good novel or business book is a priority.

Tip: A small battery backup is also nice to have. Not all aircraft have a place to recharge your devices.

The way you pack will impact the way you fly. Where are you going to put your stuff while on the plane? In most cases, you will only have access to your personal bag while in flight. Most people place their personal bags at their feet under the seat in front of them. The larger your personal bag, the less space you have for your legs and feet.

Just in case there's enough room in the overheads, I try to pack my tablet, books, headphones, and a credit card for inflight purchases in a drawstring bag that is placed inside my backpack (personal bag). By separating these items, I can pull the drawstring out and place it under the seat while putting the backpack in the overhead compartment. By placing my backpack in the overhead compartment with my carry-on, I avoid the potential of the passengers in front of me spilling their drinks on my computer and other personal items.

Many times, the overhead is full, but the backpack will flatten out enough to fit on top of the carry-on so I'm not taking up extra space. The drawstring that's placed under the seat in front of me allows me access to my entertainment during the flight. If there is simply not enough room in the overhead for both items, I am forced to place the entire personal bag under the seat in front of me. On some airlines when you upgrade your seat you also get dedicated overhead space. Be respectful to the other passengers on full flights and do not take up more than your share of space in the overhead compartment.

HERE'S WHAT'S IN MY CARRY-ON

To protect your devices, you should always plug your electronics into a power surge strip. Since there's a voltage change, we will need a travel adaptor for this trip. These adapters often include built-in surge protection as a bonus. The adaptor will go in my carry-on just in case I need to charge my devices at the airport. I like the brick ones with multiple outlets and USB ports. This allows me to charge and protect multiple devices at the same time. I will also bring a charging brick that is in my drawstring bag for easy access, not all aircraft have plugs for USB chargers, some still have the 2-prong plug, and some have no power options, hence the battery charger.

Overnight items

Toothpaste and travel soaps are placed in a small clear zip-lock plastic bag for security purposes. The zip-lock bag is placed in my backpack for easy access. Bar soaps are great during travels and don't have to be pulled out for security inspections.

Tip: I recommend placing all liquids in a zip-lock bag, even those in your checked luggage. The pressure changes on the aircraft can cause them to explode. I also loosen the cap and push out a bit of air before tightening it back up. This allows room for expansion during the pressure changes.

Make sure to check the allowable sizes of liquids and the total amount you can fly with. Each country has different requirements. TSA makes the rules and requirements for the United States, allowing 3.4 oz of liquid per container in one quart-sized clear plastic zip bag. All my liquids must fit in this ONE bag and need to be removed from my carry-on or backpack during the security check.

I do a lot of travel talks and interviews. During a recent show with April and Cindy from The Travel

Collective, we talked about airline travel and the liquid limits. If you have not followed these fellow travelers, I would highly recommend it. They have a killer YouTube channel with all kinds of travel videos. You can join in on their coffee talks. They even do a lot of travel tour interviews allowing you to educate yourself before you book your adventures. Scan the code to check out the interviews:

The problem I brought up in one of our interviews was, the cost of bug spray in Central America. There's such a big price difference that I usually check a bag just so I can bring multiple bottles. Viruses like Chikungunya, Dengue, and Zika are nothing to mess around with. To prevent these viruses, mosquito repellent is a must. From The Travel Collective, I learned that I could buy mosquito repellent in a solid bar form. With this travel hack, I can pack it in my carry-on and not worry about the liquid size. I have not been able to try this one out;

however, I look forward to it on my next trip where I might encounter these blood-sucking insects. This traveler can't wait to try out solid bar mosquito repellant.

Overnight List

No matter how much planning gets put into a trip, there is always a chance that something will happen. More than once, I have experienced an unexpected overnight stop on my travels. Therefore, I always make sure to have an overnight bag packed in my carry-on.

These are the items needed for overnight:

- Socks
- Shirt and yoga pants
- Travel toothbrush
- Pajamas (Something comfy to sleep in that covers me.)
- Undergarments
- Hairbrush
- Personal pillow (Many airlines allow a pillow. I usually carry my travel pillow in this place. A good night of sleep never happens for me on a hotel pillow. If I have a checked bag, my normal pillow from my bed at home gets packed. If no checked bag, I carry the bigger pillow instead of my

travel one or give up room in the carry-on
to ensure the pillow makes the trip.)

The overnight items ensure that if I get stuck or bags get lost, I have something appropriate to sleep in whether at a hotel or the gate while I wait for the next flight. In addition, I have fresh socks and a shirt to wear the next day. Feeling refreshed after a long day of travel can make the next part of the journey more enjoyable.

What are you wearing during your travels?

I have found wearing good shoes when traveling helps. I love my Teva flip-flops and Chuck Taylor Converse sneakers. They both come with me on every trip; however, airlines have dress codes and don't always allow flip-flops or open-toe shoes.

Many airlines even say leggings are not allowed. No airline has ever said anything to me, and I wear them often, but I have heard of other travelers having more problems lately. Keep in mind, if the airline upgrades travelers, you are more likely to get a better seat if you're dressed the part compared to a person who is in sweatpants or leggings. If I dress up for travel on the red-eye I usually put on something more comfortable after dinner is served.

A heavy jacket will be packed in the checked bag. It can also get chilly on a flight, so most of the time I wear a hoodie to keep me warm. It's easy to take off and tie around my waist or put in one of the bags. However, if there's a chance of rain both a rain jacket and hoody will be packed in my carry-on. This way if bags go missing, I have something warm and water-proof to wear.

Water Bottle

Staying hydrated is important and buying an expensive bottle of water at the airport is not on my list of things to spend my money on. I would rather spend my money on a glass of wine at our destination.

To clarify, the bottle should be empty until you pass through airport security. After the checkpoints, airports have water fountains and bottle-filling stations. Be sure to fill your water bottle before you board. There is no telling how long you may be waiting on the tarmac to take off. If a flight has a lot of turbulence, there might not be a drink service. Nowadays, many airlines have restricted services and may not even offer in-flight beverages. If you want a little flavor, you can always pack a single serving of dry drink packets.

In many countries, if you are flying onward, you must go back through security after immigration. Remember to dump your bottle out before going back through the checkpoint or you will have a problem.

There are several water bottle options. I prefer the Yeti with a screw cap because it protects the area where my lips touch and the insulation keeps my drink cold. I usually clip it to my backpack with a carabiner.

Snack

I always pack a snack. A bag of chips or crackers is nice to have when you get hungry. Most of the time my snacks are packed in my backpack/drawstring for easier access. Depending on bag size and travel times they sometimes end up in the carry-on. You can read more about what snacks are prohibited in the Customs and Immigration chapter.

CHECKED BAG

Now, this is the part where I usually stand back and evaluate my luggage and travel plans. If my travels are short or I have access to a washer and dryer I will try my hardest to pack everything in my backpack and carry-on. I hate checking and carrying big bags during my travels, but sometimes it is necessary and there is no way to avoid it.

The first thing to go in my checked bag is the travel scale. For all flights of this trip, my tickets allow 35 pounds for my carry-on and 50 pounds for the checked bag. I will need to weigh my bags before the travel begins and on our return. Keep in mind souvenirs take up space and add weight. The heavy blankets I bought for $10 each in Mexico were awesome gifts but cost me an extra $150 in over-weight bag fees.

What's going to be packed in the big bag all depends on my holiday plans. If we are planning on going to any temples, churches, mosques, or even some theaters and museums, we must keep in mind the dress codes. Many of these places will require me to cover my legs and shoulders or to wear a skirt below my knees. Some might say I even need closed-toe shoes, but they can't be sneakers. If my husband is going to accompany me, he might need a collared shirt or even a tie or suit jacket.

Since it's autumn, it's going to be chilly, if not cold. Even though a couple of the nudist beaches are on my list to experience, I don't see myself wearing a bathing suit or being topless for a long time on a cold beach. However, the hotel pools and hot tubs are on the list so my swimsuit will be included in my clothing items.

Assuming you will not have access to laundry facilities, you will need to ensure you pack enough clean options to last the duration of your trip. An alternate option is to pack detergent and hand wash your items in the sink. I don't know about you, but doing laundry is not my idea of a vacation. My priority is to pack enough clothing so that I will not be forced to wash what I take. This is almost impossible on a 30-day trip. I will need to find a laundromat or accommodations that have access to laundry services.

Tip: The things I have found that help me pack more items and keep me organized are packing cubes. I hate having to dig through my entire suitcase to locate the items I need. In addition, I can take my toiletries and shower items out in one cube and place it in the bathroom where I'll be using the items. I love my packing cubes because they allow me to stay organized and pack more. Caution, using space-saving bags like the ones you push the air out of can save a lot of space; however, with the clothing compressed, it is easy for your bag to become overweight.

Any extra bag room might be used for clothing or accessories like shoes. I try to keep my more expensive stuff like cameras in my carry-on. I want to keep as much room in my checked bag free for travel souvenirs. If you want to lock your bags, you must use a TSA lock. I can't tell you how many times the locks on my suitcase have got stuck or broken during my travels. To stop this from happening I like to use a TSA luggage strap for my checked bags.

Tip I recommend a short luggage strap or bungee that will allow you to secure your personal bag or carry-on to your large suitcase. By connecting your luggage together, you are able to transport more bags through the airport easier.

ACCESS TO LOST STUFF

I have been blessed when it comes to checking bags. Out of decades of travel, the airlines have not lost my luggage yet, but I always pack a change of clothes in my carry-on just in case. My husband cannot say the same. He has been stuck in foreign countries with only the contents of his carry-on bag to sustain him. Being able to freshen up or have sleep clothes if there's an unforeseen layover or lost bags can make a big difference in the way you feel when traveling both mentally and physically.

All my bags, even my carry-on, have a tag with my home address and a tag with my destination address. If the airline loses my bag on the way to Italy, I want them sent to my destination spot, not my home. I also put a business card on the inside of my phone and computer case just in case it ends up misplaced. If an honest person finds my items, they will know to whom they belong and how to return them to me.

Occasionally, free bags and free miles can be

redeemed if your bags are delayed. Delta is even guaranteeing bags for miles to eligible passengers, *"if your checked bag doesn't arrive at the carousel in 20 minutes or less after any domestic flight, you are eligible to receive 2,500 bonus miles"*. If flying on Delta Airlines, make sure you are a SkyMiles member at the time of travel and you must turn in a claim within three days of travel to receive any free miles. Once again make sure to read the small print (Travel).

You can even track your bags through most airlines. These are some really cool things that technology has to offer. If you are concerned about losing your luggage and don't trust the airlines, for around $20, you can purchase a little tracking device to throw in each bag.

Tip: All my luggage stands out, it's not the normal black and gray bag. You can wrap things around your bags like colored duct tape or bandanas to help make them stand out. Always check the tag has your name even if your bag is uncommon. I never thought having the same luggage would happen to me. I had a bright green suitcase with a pink bandana, who else in the world would have a combo like that? Well, I found her on a trip to Belize. It was quite a laugh when we ended up with each other's bags. Thankfully, we realized the swap as we waited in the Customs line.

THE NIGHT BEFORE

My bags are packed, my travel clothing has been laid out for the morning, and all my paperwork is ready for the 11 am flight. I have double checked there will be enough time for my ride to get me to the airport. Denver International Airport (DIA) says I should check in 2 hours before an international flight; however, security has taken me over 2 hours before. Once again, I don't like to feel rushed and I'm checking a bag. I will make sure to arrive at the airport approximately 3 hours early, this allows for extra time during checking-in or traffic problems.

Tip: If I didn't have a checked bag, I would most likely check-in online when I get to the airport. The airline starts sending emails and app alerts asking you to check in online about 24-48 hours in advance. The upside to checking in early is you might be able to buy an upgraded seat for cheap; however, I have never been able to get a clear answer from the airlines about what happens if I do an early check-in and then need to cancel my flight. Early check-in can be nice but not something I would do until I'm at the airport, just in case the car breaks down on the way or I wake up sick. There are a million other things that can happen before I leave, all are reasons to have travel insurance.

TRAVEL SAFETY

Safety when traveling is really something that should be the first thing we think about. How safe is the country(s) we are visiting? Who will we be sharing our travel plans with? How will we share our experiences and communicate with our loved ones back home? All these things need to be taken into consideration.

BIG PICTURE

Obviously, you should research the countries and cities you will be visiting. With the smallest amount of research, it is easy for a foreigner to see that New York City, New York has far more crime and is a much more dangerous place than Loveland,

Colorado. But there are other things to consider when learning about your destination.

Consider the government relations between that country and your own. Should a disaster happen, how much will your visiting country help you get home? What about the neighbors of your destination? In recent years many people visited Ukraine. How many considered an invasion from the north while on vacation? Be sure you understand the political climate of the area you are visiting and have a plan should your dream vacation become a nightmare.

Once you've established the outside risks, such as government and social stability, you need to take some time to consider what steps you can take to protect yourself on a smaller scale. Obviously, as an individual you have little impact on international relations; however, when it comes to preventing becoming a victim of crime, there are many things we can do.

Pay attention! I know this may seem a bit boring and a lot of common sense, but for some reason when we travel, we often get caught up in the moment and don't use our common sense. Other actions seem benign but can end up being quite costly.

WHO'S LISTENING?

I know you want to talk about how cool your trip is going to be, and you even might want to brag a little about the upgraded room and all the inclusive packages you bought. I get it, we work hard to pay for our travels. Seeing the world is thrilling and most of us want to talk about it. However, the world is full of not-so-nice people. Over the decades of travel, I have learned that these bad people look just like everyone else; and trust me, they are listening.

To the young girls who are traveling for the first time to Mexico. I know you are excited. However, in the first three minutes of your conversation on the flight you have told the 20 surrounding strangers where you will be staying. You talked all about the excursions you will be taking and the restaurants you plan to enjoy. As a mother and fellow traveler; this scares the hell out of me.

To the solo traveler on your way to Scotland who just wants to make conversation with the person next to them, I have no intentions of stalking you tonight. However, the strange man next to me might; and now he knows not only that you will be tasting a variety of Scotch but also what time you will be in the hotel bar.

To the mission leader who is talking about the work your team will do after you land in Nicaragua, it sounds like you will be helping others as you build homes and feed the hungry. However, as you talked about your trip to me you also told the criminal who was sitting in the seat behind us about the hostel where you and the 20 youth kids will be staying. As soon as you land, he will be calling his buddies in the kidnapping ring to make plans to round you up. A group of American kids should bring a good payout.

KNOW YOUR CONTACTS

A seemingly nice young man on one of my flights told a couple of girls he would have his friend who drives a taxi pick them up after they cleared customs. He was so nice he was even going to make sure his friend gave them a discounted fair. I was the scared mother who stopped them in the bathroom and confronted them, pleading that they make their own arrangements. They were so focused on the discount that I gave them money for a regular cab fare. It is true that there are good people in this world and that the man may have been truly trying to help. However, in this area of the world, it was common that he would call his friend who never had planned on driving the girls anywhere except to the jungle where they could have their way with them.

As a fellow traveler, I have even made the mistake

of over-sharing. All I can say is limit the conversation and things you share. Try to steer the conversation away from your plans and more toward general topics. When trying to meet people during travel, always make arrangements to meet them in a public place and be aware of your surroundings. The number one rule is don't talk about it. What you are doing and where you will be spending your time should not be shared on the flight or with the stranger next to you.

LIVING IN THE MOMENT

Did it really happen if it's not posted to social media? When I first started traveling, I shared everything I was doing in real-time. It's a rookie mistake, I was not even thinking about safety, just that I was doing something cool and wanted to share it with my friends and family back home.

It took me becoming a travel author and social media blogger to find out that what I was doing was really dangerous. Reality hit me the day my security guard in Costa Rica came to my door holding one of my books in his hand. This was the first time, but would not be the last that he would inform me people were standing at my gate who wanted to know if they could get their book autographed.

They were aware I was in Tamarindo because I had posted on social media the day before about flying into Liberia. If you looked at my social media page, it's not hard to find where I was staying. It doesn't take being in the public spotlight for someone to track and find you on social media.

You may be saying to yourself, "I'm a nobody, who would want to stalk me?" Well, if you look like you may have money or nice things, social media is the easiest way to find out where you are staying and what you are doing. With that information, it is easy for criminals to track you down and take what they want from you. All it takes is simply looking over your shoulder and identifying your profile as you post that pic of you and your bestie having the time of your life. Heck, nowadays we even give this info to strangers and tell them to follow us.

It's now a rule of thumb that I don't post when and where I'm traveling until it has happened. It may be a day, a week, or more before I post my travels on my social media. Living in the moment is being fully immersed in the experience. You cannot do that if your focus is on your phone rather than the amazing sights, sounds, and smells of this incredible world. Safety first, social media can and will wait until after the fun is had.

YOU'RE WEARING WHAT?

My grandmama would tell me that travel, and especially airline travel, is for the elite and should be accompanied by our best bags, best dress, best jewelry, etc.

I have traveled wearing designer clothing and I have traveled in sweatpants. I will tell you that I get treated differently by virtually everyone when I dress up. People seem to be nicer and more willing to help; however, this comes at a cost. What you wear can make you a target.

I don't think a bag or ring would have registered to me as being dangerous when I was young, but they can be. This is something I struggle with because I love my designer bags and like to travel with them. But just like my jewelry, they label me as a target.

One way to protect yourself should you be a victim of theft is to have it insured. Some travelers' insurance policies include theft of personal items but not all. I have an insurance policy specifically for my jewelry so if I ever end up in a position of a stickup, I will just hand it over. Although it has immense personal value, my life is not worth a ring.

Bags and even cameras are things that I think twice about packing or showing off if they do make the trip. This can be hard when packing and picking out outfits. I always travel with my jewelry on me or in my carry-on just like my cameras. None of these items of value will be in checked bags.

With a little forethought and a little restraint, you can travel with peace of mind. Do your research and know about the places you intend to visit. Share your travel plans and experiences on a need-to-know basis only. Pay attention to how you are presenting yourself and to your surroundings. Practicing these habits will help keep you safe as you experience the world and create unforgettable memories.

AIRPORT SECURITY

*W*hat's the most hated part of travel? You guessed it, airport security also known as TSA in the U.S. Realizing it's a despised part of travel, the agents assigned to this task often take a lot of flak. Try to remember that their job is to keep us safe. It is not some plot to inconvenience us. They are not simply jealous and trying to keep us from our holiday. They have a job to do and usually that job results in disgruntled passengers. Please try to be nice to them. The best way to help them is by paying attention and following their instructions. If you are kind to them and do as they instruct, there is a better chance of them being pleasant to you in return.

Most of the time security is easy, it's just that the

line takes forever. The primary reason the lines are long is that many travelers are unprepared. Once you've made it to the front of the line, if you are ready the security inspection should be quick.

Your airline ticket and ID/passport will be checked first, then you move to the scanning process. The requirements change depending on several factors including airport policy, recent events, travel threats, and even the agents working the screening area.

These are the common practices for security screening based on the majority of my trips. Jackets and shoes need to come off, and the computer and liquids must be removed from the carry-on bags and placed in the bins. Watches, belts, pocket change, vapes, or e-cigarettes should all be removed and put in a bin. With your items on the conveyor to the X-ray machine, you walk through the metal detector and pick your items up on the other side.

I would like to note that removing computers and other electronics along with removing your shoes are the most inconsistent requirements. If you are prepared to remove them, it will not be an issue if they are not required. But if you're not ready, the travelers behind you will not be happy when they are waiting on you. The bottom line is to read the signs and listen to the agents' instructions. Following directions will avoid delays.

There is an option to avoid the long security lines at over 200 airports, you just have to apply for a TSA PreCheck. If you do a lot of international travel I would recommend checking into Global Entry, it's another way to bypass security lines when returning state-side (What).

Run by the Department of Homeland Security, these application processes can take over 90 days. Government background checks and forms must be filled out. Even an interview must be done. For PreCheck, the new application fee has been lowered from $85 to $78 and a $70 online renewal that's good for five years (TSA,2022). At this time, the application for Global Entry is running $100 non-refundable. This is $22 more than PreCheck and it includes all the PreCheck benefits plus the international side.

BONUS CREDIT CARD HACK

This is another area where your credit card may offer travel benefits. My Capital One Venture card will be used, once again saving me time and money. Within two billing cycles, I will be credited up to $100 back when applying for either of these programs. It's a no-brainer between PreCheck or Global Entry. Take advantage of the money and let's go Global (TSA,2023).

Once I receive my Global Entry, I will save hours by not having to show up at the airport early because I'm able to skip the long security lines. With the special pass, my shoes get to stay on my feet, the computer and liquids never have to leave the bag, and I can keep my light jacket on. Time will also be saved when returning to my home soil by avoiding the long security lines.

Where to apply: https://tsaenrollmentbyidemia. tsa.dhs.gov/programs/precheck?

DON'T FREAK OUT!

When my husband Steve was doing his read of this book, he asked if I really wanted to include this chapter. This book was written to empower you and help you, not to frighten you of travel. He informed me that this chapter might be a scary horror story to many. Out of hundreds of trips, it was a once-in-a-lifetime thing and the chance of having something like this happen again are minimal.

After a lot of thought, I decided not to cut it, because the reality is that this was my scariest time during a security check. The point I want to make is the way I handled it. If I had freaked out, I could have been placed on the no-fly list, detained longer, and even faced crimes on foreign soil.

Heading back to the United States from Costa Rica, I was pulled out of the boarding line. My family had already gone through the main security check at the Liberia airport. A "random security search" is what they called it as we boarded the aircraft. Like the other half dozen travelers, I was pulled out of line to be tested and searched. Although random checks happen to me all the time, this was my first time being searched after clearing the security area. I remember my husband laughing as they escorted me to the other line down the hall. Steve is always giving me a hard time that I'm holding him up in security. Waving goodbye, he and my parents continued their early boarding.

This was not just the normal extra pat down and opening of bags. Each of us that was selected from the boarding line was assigned to an agent who escorted us and our carry-on baggage to a mobile inspection station. I was standing at the table as my bags, shoes, and hands were wiped down with wet cloths. I was instructed to take all my electronic devices out of their carrying case as they wiped each article. Every passenger who was pulled out was going through the same check. It has always been my approach that I have nothing to hide; open it, search it, take it all apart, get up in my personal space, and pat me down if you must.

That doesn't mean I don't stress a little as they dig through my bags. Mostly because it took hours to pack the bag perfectly and I have no clue how I'm going to get all the crap repacked in just a couple of seconds. Remember, I'm trying to board, and my plane is leaving soon. Adding a little more stress, this time there was a machine beeping every time they placed a wipe in it. The eighth wipe was the last wipe they had to do. The officer ran this final wipe across my computer keyboard. The green light and chirp were replaced with red flashing lights as the computer started a rapid loud beeping.

What happened next scared me to death. The officer carrying the automatic weapon walked over and instructed me in Spanish to place my hands on the table and sit down in the chair!

Frozen in place, my first words were, "No hablo español, English por favor." Another officer with a bigger gun repeated what he said in English.

As an experienced traveler, I know what's packed in my bags and there's nothing that should hold me up. The rules of thumb are don't freak out, answer the questions as best as you can, and follow their instructions. I cautiously placed my hands on the table as my bare feet moved the rest of my body quickly to the chair that I had been instructed to sit in.

The armed guard asked me my name and occupation in Spanish. I could understand what he was asking but just to be sure, I had the man who was interpreting in English repeat it. Spanish is not my native tongue and now is not the time to be practicing a second language.

I was told to take my hair down and place the tie in the tray. Then I was instructed to remove my wedding ring and earrings and place them in the same tray. The officer informed me to place my hands back on the table as two more people came over and started wiping my bags again. They ensured they both wiped all sides of the bags and what was placed in the tray. They inspected a few random items in each bag. I also got a full pat down from head to toe.

It took an extra 30 minutes, as they wiped and placed each piece in a different computer to be scanned. I tried not to speak too much, but I did ask a couple of questions. The officers told me some sunscreens, lotions and even hair products can make the computer beep. After the trip, I did some follow-up research on what might cause it to beep since I was not carrying drugs. My research shows some skin and hair products can leave traces of glycerin which can cause a false positive. They were checking for chemicals that could be used in explosives (Helmen-stine). I will never again use another baby wipe when cleaning my computer keys before traveling.

Once again, I had nothing to hide so I just let them do some more wiping and taking apart my bags. There is no feeling like that of holding up a whole international flight. I was the fourth person in line to board the flight, but in the end, I was the last person to walk on board. Since only a plexiglass wall separated us, everyone behind me also watched the scene play out as they boarded. If that wasn't bad enough, additional passengers were pulled out of line for inspection due to my beep.

Sounds terrible, right? Let's break this down. The officers had a passenger fail their chemical test. They held the flight to ensure the safety of everyone onboard. After following procedures until they were confident there was no threat, they allowed me to board, and the flight to proceed. It was unfortunate the process delayed the flight forty-five minutes but that's a small price to pay to ensure the safety of a few hundred passengers.

Sure, it was stressful and embarrassing for me, but again, it's about the safety of everyone. By not losing my cool and following instructions I prevented further delay and suspicion. Remember, having a breakdown can land you on the no-fly list. The officers were able to complete their procedures quickly and get the plane cleared for takeoff.

Remember, this is just part of the process. These people are trying to keep us safe in the air and in our homelands after arriving. Know the rules and follow instructions. Leave plenty of time to get through the checkpoint and to the next gates. Don't carry or watch other people's bags. Most importantly, don't freak out and keep calm.

AIRPLANE ETIQUETTE

*T*he first and foremost rule of airplane etiquette is to be nice to the flight attendants.

Do you know most of those flight attendants and even the pilots are not getting paid when they greet you during boarding? On many airlines helping passengers get settled, placing heavy suitcases in overhead bins, or even passing out drinks to first-class patrons doesn't count, the flight crew's pay doesn't start until the cabin doors are closed.

Passing out little gift bags is a small way to say thank you to the Pilots and Flight Attendants. It's never a requirement; just an act of kindness. I wish I could say this was my idea; however, it came from a travel group on Facebook I follow called "Girls Love Travel".

Talk about some creative travelers! I have seen all kinds of gifts. The gift doesn't have to be expensive; some have little candies, packs of gum, hand wipes, or even ChapSticks. Other bags I have seen cost more with gift cards to places like Starbucks or even little keychains. You can get all kinds of creative with these gifts. The number of crew changes depending on the type of aircraft. Just do a quick search for the aircraft you are flying on to see how many bags you will need. I put all the gifts in one bag and give it to one of the attendants as I board the flight. This way I don't hold up the line during boarding. They will pass out the bags to the rest of the crew when it's convenient for them.

DO YOU RECLINE ON AIRPLANES?

Do you recline on airplanes? This is a hot travel question, and the answer is it depends on whom you ask. If you ask me, I say yes, as a matter of fact, absolutely!

A lot of travelers disagree with me believing it's rude. Even the CEO of Delta, Ed Bastian stated, *"it's an etiquette issue ... if a passenger knows a tall person is sitting behind them, they should ask permission before they recline"* (Staff).

I'm usually the first passenger with my seat back in the reclining position. I booked my comfort according to my travel needs when I purchased the seat. Most people will be in a reclined position, so I understand what that means to me if I buy the seat behind them. I fully expect the seatback to be over my legs.

If you don't want to be behind a reclining seat, then buy an upgrade or a bulkhead seat. A bulkhead seat doesn't have a seat in front of it, instead, you're facing a wall or have an open emergency space giving you a little extra room. There is a tradeoff, since you lose the seat in front you also lose the spot to place your personal bag at your feet. This can make it hard to get to my drawstring/backpack that has my electronics packed in them. You can't hold a bag during take-off or landing, and the aisle must be clear of items. If you fly this way you will have to wait until the fastened seat belt light is turned off so you can stand up and access the overhead compartment.

You can also fly Spirit Airline where the seats don't recline, just remember to look at their bag sizes and fees. From check-in fees to food and drinks, there's a fee for everything and they can add up quickly. On these flights, you can save money by checking in online and printing tickets at home while traveling with only a small bag. When prepared and packed properly, I have flown with Spirit on many shorter flights and never had a bad experience. For most of my longer flights, I'm looking for comfort and the ability to carry more bags than I'm allowed on most of the cheaper airlines like American or Spirit. Once again, it all depends on how much I can spend and what luxuries I want to travel with.

Over the years I've spent thousands of dollars on major airlines like Delta and United. I'm part of their miles programs and both airlines fall in my top two favorite domestic carriers. Over the last three decades of travel, I've had the pleasure of flying with them on many occasions. I have bought tickets in basic, main, comfort, business, and even first-class.

When booking a flight, I give my seating a lot of thought since it affects two major things when I travel, my bank account and my comfort. Let me tell you Mr. Bastian, your inches and reclining seats have cost me a lot of money!

A LITTLE SPACE MAKES A BIG DIFFERENCE

I learned at a very young age that having a nice seat while traveling makes a BIG difference. My seat and inches will play a big role in my bank account and how I feel when I arrive at my destination. This can cost me time and money. Two things I take very seriously.

When I travel for business, a bigger seat can make the difference in being able to show up refreshed for a business meeting or presentation. It can mean having enough room to pull my laptop out so that I can work on my next project that might be due in a couple of hours. This can be very challenging in a smaller seat where there's not even enough room for me, let alone the person who just reclined in my lap.

When I'm traveling on holiday, my seat makes a difference. If I show up jet lagged and hurting from my flight, it will affect how relaxing my vacation is. Reclining on airplanes is a must to be able to stretch out and even catch a little shuteye. I don't know about you, but I want to enjoy my travels, not wish I had stayed home.

HOW MUCH IS AN INCH WORTH TO YOU?

To me, it can be priceless. Let's face it, traveling can be uncomfortable. Challenges like cancellations, long flights, layovers, and hours of standing in lines can take the fun out of traveling. Added stress comes from small uncomfortable seats that have limited space for me and my belongings. This all can lead me to feel physically and emotionally drained during and after my travels.

Understanding how much an inch is going to cost me has been crucial when booking my seats. This is going to affect all my travels, so I want to make the right decision. In the end, it can cost me thousands of dollars for that extra couple of inches.

Understanding Inches

For those of you who don't understand how Delta charges for inches let me explain. I'm currently in Costa Rica and I want to fly stateside in March. I'm going to fly out of Liberia Costa Rica (LIR) to Denver International Airport (DIA).

The cheapest ticket for Delta that day is $377. This is a Basic ticket meaning my seat is not assigned until after I check in. I have no clue how much room I'm going to have. I do know that the seat in front of me will most likely be reclined and this is going to affect my space and can make my travels uncomfortable.

1st UPGRADE - For an additional charge of $36.90 I can upgrade to what Delta refers to as "Main". This gets me advanced seating while also allowing me to pick my seat from the available seats in the main section. These seats recline while offering standard legroom. Just like Basic, there's a high likelihood the passenger in the seat in front of me will be reclined. This is a small upgrade, but it allows me to pick from a small section of seats making sure that I don't get the dreaded back row. You know, the ones that don't recline right next to the bathroom. I like the aisle so I can stand and go to the bathroom without climbing over people. The window is also nice because I can rest my pillow against it and also enjoy the view. This upgrade keeps me from being placed in the dreaded middle seat. If I'm traveling with people, this will allow us to book seats together. If we book the cheaper option, my travel buddy and I might be separated.

2nd Upgrade - If I want more room, I might want to think about spending an additional $88.60 so I can enjoy what they call "Comfort" seating. This gives me up to 3 inches of extra legroom. I'm paying Delta Airlines $41.83 for every inch over the basic ticket price. This upgrade gives me more legroom and a reclining seat. My goal when taking this upgrade is to book a seat that reclines behind a non-reclining seat. This allows me the most space and no reclining seat in front of me. Usually, these are the seats that sit behind the ones over the wing. This section of seats is in an emergency exit row, they don't recline and like bulkheads don't have a place for your bags. The legroom in these seats is great but you also need to be physically able and willing to help if there's an emergency.

Tip: If you're looking to avoid turbulence over the wing or at the front of the aircraft is the best seat. If you are like me and want to stretch out, make sure you are not in an emergency exit row. Ensure your seat reclines at the time of booking.

3rd Upgrade - If that is still not enough room, I can upgrade to "First Class". First Class will give me an additional 8 inches of legroom and a reclining seat. These 8 inches are going to cost me $1,135.30. Bringing the grand total to $1,546 which means I'm paying $141.91 for every inch of extra space.

Are you willing to give up comfort? Sometimes, my comfort and sleep are worth more than a cheap ticket. If I have long travel times an extra 3-8 inches of legroom and a reclining seat can be extremely valuable to me. The small seats in the back of the aircraft are hard to get comfortable in. On long travels, it can be a nightmare without reclining on airplanes. I have paid thousands of dollars in upgrade fees to make sure that I have enough room to be comfortable.

If the traveler behind me needs more room when my seat is in a reclined position, they need to buy an upgrade. This is their problem, not mine. I paid for the seat and the inches that the airline offered me when I booked my ticket.

To all you fellow travelers who believe I'm being rude or that I should ask before I recline, all I can say is, I will not ask for permission to use the inches I paid for as a traveler. I expect the person in front of me is going to recline at one time or another just like me. Just in case I have liquids or devices on the tray, I appreciate it when the person in front of me reclines slowly. It's nice but rare when they inform me they are moving their chair back. Often the seat back falls into my lap, and I scramble to secure the items on the tray.

So once again, how much is an inch worth to you? Are you willing to give up some comfort and risk having someone reclined into your lap to save money? This is a personal question that each traveler should ask themselves before booking any flight.

The Value of an Inch

Main	Comfort	First-class
$36.90	$88.60	$1,135.30
(Reclining)	$41.83/inch	$141.91/inch

AIRPORT CUSTOMS AND IMMIGRATIONS

*W*hen do you go through customs and immigration? Customs and Immigration inspection can happen anytime the tires of a plane touch another country's territory. If you have layovers in different countries these processes could happen multiple times on an international trip. Not all countries require connecting flights to pass through these checkpoints, but most do. You should know what each country expects before you begin your travels. Be prepared, remember every country has different rules.

In addition to foreign customs and immigration, most countries will require travelers to pass back through a security checkpoint before boarding their next flight. Remember to empty your water bottle or any other liquids you may have picked up along the way.

Since our first layover is in the U.S. followed by a red-eye flight to Italy, we will not go through customs until we touch down in Florence (FCO). The return flight is slightly different as we will go through Immigration and Customs when we touch down in the U.S. for the first time.

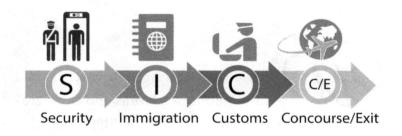

Security Immigration Customs Concourse/Exit

ARE YOU PREPARED FOR IMMIGRATION AND CUSTOMS

When I pack my bags, I want to make sure both myself and the bags I'm bringing are ready for Immigration and Customs inspection. This is just part of the process. It's nothing to fear; however, passing through these checkpoints can feel overwhelming if you are not prepared. Honestly, I still think my blood pressure goes up every time I pass through a checkpoint. I do a few things to make the immigration and customs process as smooth as possible.

UNDERSTAND THE FORMS

I like to view the Immigration and Customs Declaration forms online before I travel, this helps me be prepared. Some countries have gone to an automated system where you scan your passport and answer questions on a computer screen after you deboard the aircraft; while others still require you to complete paper forms. The process varies slightly from country to country. Some will require one form for Immigration and a separate form for Customs Declaration. Other countries combine both into one form. A quick Google search of the country and travel forms will get you the standard questions. You are also able to view the forms you will need to complete.

Tip: When my minor child did her first international trip without an adult, we filled the forms out together before she traveled. She carried a printed copy with the answers completed with her other travel documents. This way she could just copy the information onto the original form.

YOU DON'T WANT TO BREAK THE RULES!

What does the country allow? Not all countries will allow certain prescriptions or even some of the over-the-counter medications available in the U.S. If you are traveling with any medication, make sure to check that it is allowed in all countries you will visit and pass through. When traveling with prescriptions, ensure they are in the original labeled bottles. Be sure the prescription is not expired, and that the name matches the name on your identification.

Not all foods are allowed. I learned this on an international trip when a group of us forgot our travel host had packed lunches to eat on the flight. These lunches each had an apple in them. When our group started to go through Customs inspection in the Dominican Republic our bags were X-rayed. The customs agents started pulling the people I was traveling with aside.

The travelers like me who had not eaten the apples on the flight still had them in their bags. I was lucky enough to be at the back of the line where I was able to dip out to the restroom and eat the fruit. The unlucky ones at the front of the line ended up paying $500 per apple. They also got held up in Customs for a little over two hours, almost costing us the last bus to our accommodations.

Although each country has its own list of items prohibited from travel, there are a handful of common items that should be avoided. My rule of thumb is NO beef jerky or sunflower seeds; two of my favorite things when traveling. Don't pack fruits, nuts, seeds, meats, or vegetables unless you plan on eating them before you land. Weapons of all types are prohibited to be carried on and there are additional requirements and restrictions for packing them in your checked bags. Some countries prohibit weapons transportation of any kind without proper permits and/or licensing.

Adult Toys

Will the pink vibrator be packed? Never in my wildest dreams did I think I would be writing about adult toys in a travel book, but it needs to be talked about since these toys can land us behind bars. If Thailand or Vietnam were my destinations, or if a layover was in Asia, my adult toys would be left behind. The reality is, in some countries, you can be arrested for adult toys. Many countries see my pink friend as pornography or taboo and it could land me in a foreign prison, simply for trying to have a little fun on my vacation.

If it's a country that allows adult toys, it's getting packed. In the old days, I would pull out the batteries and pack the toy in my checked baggage. This helps avoid any embarrassment in the security lines. However, technology has changed and now many toys have rechargeable batteries made of lithium-ion. Just like electric cigarettes and vape pens, these items must be packed in a carry-on, and not all countries will allow them.

Tips: Make sure the toy is not charged or the batteries have been removed. Things get shifted around during travel. There's nothing like hitting turbulence and hearing your special friend start vibrating in the overhead compartment.

I always recommend checking with both the airline and TSA for items that you can bring.

https://www.tsa.gov/

CURRENCY

Coming right out of the gates, I will tell you that I would never travel with large amounts of money on me. Many countries don't have a limit on how much currency I can bring into the country. However, for the majority, you must declare cash amounts of USD $10,000 or more to customs (Money). That is way too much cash for my comfort.

If you are carrying large amounts of cash, you will most likely be stopped at the customs inspection. Yes, the x-ray machines will pick it up. If you are carrying this large amount of currency, make sure to declare it on your Customs Declaration form so you can avoid problems and the risk of having every penny seized.

Never keep your money all in one place. I always space my money out during travel. I have used pony-tail holders with compartments, my personal bag, and even a little in my carry-on. On occasion, I even put some cash in my socks, shoes, or bra. This ensures that if I lose a bag or someone pickpockets me that I have enough for taxis and food. Like always, it depends on the country and what I'm doing.

My credit cards will be used more than cash. One of the benefits my card offers is that all ATM and international exchange fees will be reimbursed. Each card number and the international phone numbers to customer service have been saved to the cloud. If my cards are lost or stolen, I will easily be able to contact the credit card company. I will also make cash-back and miles points for my purchases on my cards. Getting paid to touch the world is empowering. My credit cards offer purchaser insurance which is a bonus.

Tip: Make sure to call the credit card companies before international travel so they can make a note in your file that the card will be used outside its original country.

This helps make sure that the credit card company won't put a hold on the card due to unusual activity. It really sucks not being able to check into a hotel or pay for a meal you just ate because the card was declined due to a fraud hold. Usually, a quick call to the card company will fix the problem; however, no one wants to be on hold with a credit card company when they could be seeing the sites. Not to mention it is a bit embarrassing.

YOU ARE ONLY RESPONSIBLE FOR YOURSELF!

After landing, we will disembark with all our carry-on belongings. I will not carry the bag for the old lady or gentleman who tried to befriend me during the flight. I will not help the young woman who has a baby, or the younger kid who has become my buddy during the 14-hour journey. This is a hard one because I was always raised to help. But I can't, I won't, and I will even point out to a flight attendant or security guard if I'm asked to help anyone in this kind of capacity. The only bags that will come with me are mine.

This is a safety issue. The people who were strangers 14 hours before my flight might feel like friends, but the reality is they are strangers. Even when traveling with a mission team where I know my fellow travelers and we have trained for months before our trip, their bags are their bags, not mine.

It's hard to think that the 80-year-old grandma who showed me photos and tried to talk my ear off during the flight might have a weapon. Or the mother with the baby who just looks tired and needs a little help carrying the diaper bag, but what she really needs is for you to carry the drugs that she put in the baby formula through security.

Regardless of how close my fellow travelers may be, I did not pack their bags and have no clue what's in them. I am not going to be detained in Customs because my friends were not aware that the items they packed were prohibited. It may be an honest mistake, but I'm not going to pay the price for it.

The flight attendants can and will arrange help for any of these people who need it. All you need to do is press the call button on the overhead bin. If I'm asked to do this during the deboarding process it's a little harder since the attendants have moved to the front of the cabin and the walkway is full of people. The response would still be no, followed by the light being pushed and me telling them I would inform the first flight attended I walked by that they needed help. In the process, I would also make it clear to the attendant that I was not traveling with the other person. Once again this is about safety.

PAY ATTENTION

The biggest advice I can give when going through immigration and customs is to follow instructions, pay attention, listen, and read signs. The flight attendants will start giving instructions while you are still in the air. This is so important. I'm going to say it again, PAY ATTENTION! This starts even before the international flight touches down on both foreign and home soil.

In most international airports there will be signs in English. If you have problems reading signs, I recommend downloading translator apps. There are all kinds of apps that will read the signs out loud and even apps that will translate the signs into another language. Technology is our friend, make sure to download and get familiar with the apps before traveling.

IMMIGRATION

Most of the time this process starts in the air when the flight attendants begin to pass out the Immigration and Customs Declaration forms. The pen that was packed in my small fanny pack/passport carrier will be used and the extra one I have will most likely be passed around in the cabin to the many people who didn't bring one. If the country you are landing in has a digital process, you will not be given the paper forms but rather be instructed on where to access the kiosk.

> *Tip: Have your flight number handy and your destination address accessible. Flight numbers and destination addresses are usually asked for on the forms or at the checkpoint. Your address is most likely the hotel where you will be staying or the address of your vacation rental.*

For international flights, all passengers are required to disembark the plane. They must then pass through Immigration. Very few countries have had me collect my check bags before going through the immigration checkpoint.

All family members go through this checkpoint as a group when traveling together. Usually, my husband leads us. It seems to be a new rule that any passenger five years or older must carry their own passport and paperwork. As a parent, I believe it is crucial to teach our kids; however, I would never pass these documents to a child before they needed to hand them over to an officer. I would then collect all the documents after we cleared the checkpoint. I think my children were around 14 or 15 years old before I allowed them to carry their own paperwork.

In countries like the U.S. where we scan our passports into the computer on our return flight, we approach the kiosks individually. My kids seem to have mastered the system. Usually, this step of the process ends with them giving me a hard time about how quickly they can get through the checkpoint compared to me.

After we teach, we get to watch as our kids spread their wings. It's sometimes hard as our children get older and start to travel without us. However, both my younger kids traveled internationally as solo travelers at the age of 16 years old and they had to be responsible for all their government IDs and paperwork.

Most of the time the immigration officer will ask for the form that was filled out on the flight and your passport/visa. This is where they might also request your onward travel. The destination address might also be needed. I have all this information on my phone and in paper format. I usually just hand them the papers as they ask for them.

If the digital kiosk was used, it will often print out a form with your completed answers. You will need to present this form with your other documents to the immigration officer.

Only give the immigration officer what they ask for and pay attention to the signs and instructions on what page of your passport to have exposed. It seems some country's immigration officers are there just to stamp. I have seen picture pages being stamped instead of passport pages because travelers did not read the sign as they walked up to the counter.

BAGGAGE CLAIM

The next step is the baggage claim. This is where you will collect any checked luggage off the bag carousel. Even if you have a connecting flight, in most countries you must collect all of your luggage. You will re-check your bags once you have passed through customs. If we did not check bags, we get to skip this step and go straight to Customs Declaration and Inspection.

CUSTOMS

The Customs Declaration and Inspection are fairly straightforward processes. It varies from country to country and airport to airport. It can also change depending on which officers are on duty. Most of the time you will present the customs officer with your passport and declaration form. Bags are placed on scanners, and you might even be asked to line up and let the dogs walk through and smell your luggage.

If you did not declare your belongings properly or if the inspectors suspect prohibited items further investigation will commence. You will be asked about the value of your items, the amount of cash, or several other questions pertaining to what you are traveling with and where. However, most of the time the Customs Declaration and Inspection are uneventful.

PAYING TAXES AND CUSTOMS FEES

Are you buying artwork? Are my designer bag and new jewelry going to be taxed when I come back to my home country? Maybe, or maybe not; it all depends on how much we spend and what we bring into the country.

It doesn't matter if it's your home soil or a foreign territory if you are transporting goods over a certain price, you will be required to pay taxes on said items. Cigarettes and liquor are not only taxed, but they also have limits on the quantity you can bring into the U.S. For instance, you are only allowed 200 cigarettes. Depending on the brand that's about one carton of smokes. If you are going to bring back liquor, a liter is all you get.

I have been on mission trips where we have had to

pay to bring in our bags that were full of flip-flops, coloring books, and even toothbrushes. These items were donations and were going to be passed out at orphanages and to the poor; however, they were goods that we brought into the country. Once again, this all depends on the customs agent. The toothbrushes were overlooked in Belize; however, the flip flops our team brought into Nicaragua were taxed because the agents didn't like that we had a whole suitcase full.

You can try to avoid paying the fees by taking new items out of boxes and removing the price tags. The customs officers usually only focus on new items or those that were recently purchased, but this doesn't always work. Remember, if you are passing through a country's borders, not disclosing cash and new purchases is against the law and can cost you high fines and even deny your entry.

The total value of my souvenirs and designer bags needs to be under $800 or I'm going to be paying taxes to bring them home (Warning). I recommend keeping all your receipts for purchased items so that you are not overcharged on taxes.

Duty-Free

Watch the signs for the duty-free shops. This is where you get your liquor and other goods like perfume and chocolates without paying the tax. If you are flying onward, make sure when checking out of the duty-free shop that any liquids are placed in proper bags and sealed up correctly.

I still get frustrated thinking about the time the Costa Rica duty-free clerks placed my rum in a plastic sealed bag, but it didn't have the proper red label that was required at the security checkpoint in Chicago. This happened because they had run out of the newly required bags, so the clerk used the old ones. It worked just fine when boarding the plane in Costa Rica.

However, when we checked in for our next flight at security in Chicago we were stopped and told we could not carry the alcohol through because it didn't have a red security stripe on the bag. Since it was a mistake of the duty-free clerks, the security officers made an exception and pulled our bags back out so we could place the $300 worth of liquor in our checked bags instead of us having to dispose of them.

This time hold-up in security cost us our next flight. If we had not already missed the flight, I would have given the rum to the security guards as a gift just to get through the checkpoint and catch my plane. The next available flight did not leave until the following morning. Overnight in the Chicago airport and 15 hours of my time is what that amazing-tasting rum cost me.

This is why I also have access to emergency funds or a credit card when traveling. I remember Steve pointing out that we were traveling on a budget, and I had already blown that at the duty-free shop. The tickets were so cheap it was going to cost more than the airline tickets themself to put insurance on them. You guessed it, I tried to save money on my travels and here I stood with no insurance. He asked if I really wanted to tap into my miles or our emergency fund or if I was ready to sleep at the airport.

To this day I don't understand why Chicago O'Hare International Airport (ORD) doesn't offer sleep pods. Many airports around the world offer pods that usually cost less than a hotel room. The cost ranges depending on the sleeping area. Some pods charge hourly rates, others have overnight/day rates as low as $39. These pods can be a godsend when you need sleep on long travels.

If we had not been traveling on a budget, I would have paid the extra $225 for a hotel that had a free shuttle to and from the airport. Instead, my words were something stupid like, "We got this. A night in the airport is nothing, we used to do it all the time."

Looking back on that trip I should have tapped into my points or just put the room on the credit card. Maybe it's because I'm older, but sleeping on the airport floor or trying to find a bench that I can get comfortable on was impossible. Whenever we are stuck in the airport, for the security of ourselves and our belongings, only one of us sleeps at a time. Usually, we break it up into blocks so we each get a chance at some decent rest. Books are read and shows are watched on our devices as we kill time and try to relax.

Tired and grouchy is what this traveler was when we landed in Colorado. This is not the way I like to travel; however, we did make it. Other than the Rum, the crazy travel budget I had set of less than $300 for both of us to travel from Costa Rica to Colorado was still intact. We were also able to use the untouched miles to do some stateside traveling during our trip. It made the uncomfortable overnight in the airport worth it in the end.

WE MADE IT

*L*et's take stock of our preparations. We have done our research and have chosen the place we want to visit next. We have familiarized ourselves with the logistics of visiting such as language, currency, healthcare, security, etc. We have established what time of year is best for what we want to do. With our travel documents and vaccinations in hand, we searched for the best prices and accommodations for flights. We ensured our insurance needs were taken care of. Before we packed our bags, we researched security procedures to ensure we didn't take anything prohibited and that our liquids and electronics were accessible. Completing preparations with airplane etiquette and inspection processes we are now ready to board our flight.

Over the years I have experienced many amazing sites and activities. I swam with stingrays off little Caribbean islands. I performed for the Queen of England on the royal grounds. I stood on the Mayan ruins in Belize and rode horses in the canopy of the Costa Rica jungle. In Scotland, I was able to sample whiskey from around the country and tour old castles. I built homes for the poor in Nicaragua. I have even helped boys and girls who had been sold into sex trade trafficking in the Dominican Republic. These are a few parts of the world I have experienced, and I have the stamps in my passport as reminders.

Many would say I have traveled the world. As I look back at all my travels, both domestic and international, I have taken several trips. However, one thing is for sure, I have not even begun to touch this big world. There's still so much more to see and do.

I can tell you with all confidence, it feels good to get off the couch and on the plane! My passport is up to date, my tickets are booked, and my bags are packed. How about you? Who knows, maybe my next book will be an Italy Travel Guide.

To my fellow travelers, I hope the tips and tricks in this quick read save you time, money, and frustration as you experience exotic locations and interact with foreign cultures.

Now that you know what it takes to get a passport and book the tickets to another country, where will you be traveling to?

Scan the code to check out our travel links and join fellow travelers!

ABOUT THE AUTHOR

Every author has a story, and Nikki Page is no different. As co-founder of Viva Purpose, this incredible woman has created writings that instruct, educate, and entertain. As an experienced and self-proclaimed nomad, as well as an experienced writer and traveler, this woman has committed her life to educate and bring life to those who wander. Here is more about Nikki and her life's work.

#1 Internationally Best-Selling Travel Author

With books like, "Cut The Crap & Move To Costa Rica, A How-to Guide Based On These Gringos Experience" and, "The Ultimate Costa Rica Cookbook: Healthy, Quick, & Easy Meals," Nikki Page is one best-selling author who creates culturally relevant and accurate books to educate and inform her readers.

Experienced Traveler

Having spent thousands of days abroad, Nikki Page has her fair share of cultural experiences when it comes to traveling, particularly when it comes to

Central America. If you are looking for cookbooks, travel guides, and first-hand accounts of global events, you'll enjoy her work.

Historic Writer

During the COVID pandemic, Nikki got stuck in Costa Rica for a total of 228 days. Locked away from family with no chance to make it back state-side, her adventures are laid out in her book, "228 Days Trapped in Paradise: The Diary of an Expat Chica in Costa Rica." She writes her Costa Rica-educated books from experience.

Scan the code to visit Nikki Page's author page.

WORKS CITED

"Changi Airport." *Wikipedia*, Wikimedia Foundation, 26 Jan. 2023, https://en.wikipedia.org/wiki/Changi_Airport.

"Digital ID." *Digital ID | Transportation Security Administration*, https://www.tsa.gov/digital-id#:~:text=TSA%20currently%20accepts%2C%20for%20limited,Wallet%20at%20the%20airports%20below.

"Flying with Children." *Flying with Children | Federal Aviation Administration*, 15 Dec. 2022, https://www.faa.gov/travelers/fly_children.

Helmenstine, Anne Marie. "These Common Chemicals Could Get You Flagged by TSA." *ThoughtCo*, ThoughtCo, 18 Nov. 2019, https://www.thoughtco.com/chemicals-false-positive-tsa-swab-test-606808.

"Incheon Airport Korea Traditional Culture Center: 인천국제공항 한국전통문화센터." *TRIPPOSE*, 26 Feb. 2017, https://en.trippose.com/tour/incheon-airport-korea-traditional-culture-center.

Italy, Select. "Warning: Know the Customs Rules!" *It's All About Italy*, 17 Jan. 2021, https://selectitaly.com/blog/tips-travelers/warning-know-the-Customs-rules/.

"Money and Other Monetary Instruments." *U.S. Customs and Border Protection*, 12 Mar. 2020, https://www.cbp.gov/travel/international-visitors/kbyg/money.

"Programstsa Precheck®." *Universal Enrollment Services*, https://tsaenrollmentbyidemia.tsa.dhs.gov/programs/precheck.

"Requirement for Proof of COVID-19 Vaccination for Air Passengers." *Centers for Disease Control and Prevention*, Centers for Disease Control and Prevention, 30 Dec. 2022, https://www.cdc.gov/coronavirus/2019-ncov/travelers/proof-of-vaccination.html#:~:text=If%20you%20are%20a%20non,States%20from%20a%20foreign%20country.

Rodriguez, Christy. "REAL ID Act: What It Means, State by State

Requirements & Updates." *UpgradedPoints.com*, 13 Dec. 2022, https://upgradedpoints.com/travel/real-id-act/.

"Smart Traveler Enrollment Program." *U.S. Department of State*, U.S. Department of State, https://step.state.gov/step/.

Staff, TMZ. "Delta CEO Says Passengers Should Ask Permission to Recline Seat." *TMZ*, TMZ, 14 Feb. 2020, https://www.tmz.com/2020/02/14/delta-ceo-says-passengers-should-ask-permission-to-recline-seat/.

"Travel Planning Center." *Submission: 20 Minutes Baggage Claim: Delta Air Lines*, 2018, https://www.delta.com/bags/bagsClaimAutomation.action.

"TSA PreCheck® vs. Global Entry." *Capital One*, 2023, https://www.capitalone.com/learn-grow/money-management/tsa-precheck-global-entry-credit/.

"TSA Reduces TSA PreCheck® Enrollment Fee." *TSA Reduces TSA PreCheck® Enrollment Fee | Transportation Security Administration*, 4 Nov. 2022, https://www.tsa.gov/news/press/releases/2022/11/04/tsa-reduces-tsa-precheckr-enrollment-fee.

U.S. Department of State, U.S. Department of State, https://travel.state.gov/.

"What Is the Difference between Global Entry, TSA PreCheck® and the Other Trusted Traveler Programs?" *What Is the Difference between Global Entry, TSA PreCheck® and the Other Trusted Traveler Programs? | Transportation Security Administration*, 2023, https://www.tsa.gov/travel/frequently-asked-questions/what-difference-between-global-entry-tsa-precheckr-and-other.